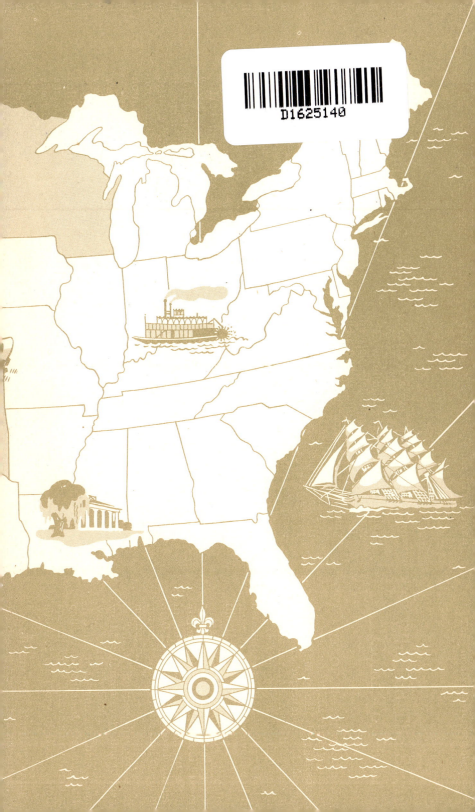

D1625140

THE COUNTY ELECTION (1851)
BY GEORGE CALEB BINGHAM (1811–1879)
In the collection of The Boatmen's National Bank

Because Stump Speaking, The County Election, and The Verdict of the People were painted by Bingham about the time that Boatmen's was established, and because they portray Missouri people of that period almost photographically, these paintings were acquired by the Bank for its collection.

THE COUNTY ELECTION (1851)
BY GEORGE CALEB BINGHAM (1811–1879)
In the collection of The Boatmen's National Bank

Because *Stump Speaking*, *The County Election*, and *The Verdict of the People*
were painted by Bingham about the time that Boatmen's was established, and
because they portray Missouri people of that period almost photographically,
these paintings were acquired by the Bank for its collection.

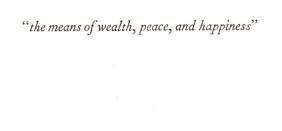

"the means of wealth, peace, and happiness"

A part of the November 9, 1847 issue of "The Republican." Mr. Chambers' editorial supplemented the new "institution's" advertisement which ran on the same day.

"the means of wealth, peace, and happiness"

~~~~~~

THE STORY OF THE OLDEST BANK

WEST OF THE MISSISSIPPI

BY W. G. RULE

1847–1947

THE BOATMEN'S NATIONAL BANK
OF SAINT LOUIS

COPYRIGHT 1947, BY
THE BOATMEN'S NATIONAL BANK
OF ST. LOUIS

Foreword

St. Louis was a village with muddy streets and no railroad, telegraph, or telephone, but it was set on a river bank crossroads where many steamboats landed. The boats brought furs, minerals, and provisions from the interior and into it they carried ever more people who would send out more and more of the products of the land.

Of all the instruments most vital to modern civilization, then lacking, the one most needed was money. The back country had sufficient natural resources; it was rapidly acquiring an energetic population. Given money, it could obtain whatever else it needed.

In all of the vast territory west of the Mississippi River no bank which started operation before October 18, 1847, has survived the intervening period. On that day the Boatmen's Saving Institution began business. On October 18, 1947, it is still active and is a more influential force in national banking than it has ever been before. It has survived robbery and fire, depression and war. Its growth has been entirely internal; there has been no accretion of resources by consolidation.

To attempt within the brief confines of these covers to say completely why these things have happened would be impossible. Boatmen's has been successful primarily because its customers have prospered. Other things which have influenced its course are set down in these pages.

Contents

List of Illustrations

"the means of wealth, peace, and happiness"

I

Background

WHEN the land which is the North American continent had been finally formed, three rivers constituted its central drainage system. These streams would later make a great inland waterway. For hundreds of years after man inhabited the great valley these paths were the only practical transportation arteries for this vast area.

By chance of topography the two laterals join the main stem within a short distance of each other, and perhaps without fully realizing the eventual significance of the arrangement, the French very early recognized the local importance of the country where the three rivers met, and made several important settlements in it.

Before its occupation by the French, over a period not accurately defined, it had been a bountiful habitat for the red men and for a short period it would be under the nominal control of Spain before its acquisition and development by "Americans."

When a modern retail store seeks a new location, it counts the passersby at its proposed site and so determines its probable custom. While the commercially minded French of New Orleans had not developed this technique to its present state, they understood quite well that all men who traveled in the great middle country eventually progressed along the strip of the Mississippi between the mouths of the Missouri and the Ohio. And so, when Pierre Laclede Liguest received from his King a

3

grant to trade with the savages west of the Mississippi and north of the Missouri, he planned to place his headquarters within that stretch of 125 miles where all men passed.

Laclede had been born in southern France, the scion of a prosperous and substantial family. Intelligent, handsome, and of sturdy physique, he possessed a commanding personality and abundant energy. Coming to New Orleans at the age of thirty-one, he quickly made friends and one of these friendships developed into a life-long connection—that with Col. Antoine Maxent. In 1762 these men pooled fortunes and influence and obtained under the name Maxent, Laclede and Company the trading grant which has been mentioned.

When the expedition left New Orleans on August 3, 1763, to establish a post for the new venture, it is unlikely that Laclede knew the sovereignty of the territory into which he was traveling. The customs of the day being what they were, Louis XV had not informed all of his subjects that he had ceded to England all claim to land east of the Mississippi, nor that he had made at least a nominal transfer of French possessions on the west bank to Spain. It is probable that not only the citizens, but official New Orleans as well, thought that France still controlled the entire valley.

Although Laclede had already determined the general location of his post, his plan was to proceed to Ste. Genevieve, a village which had been established some thirty years, where he would store his goods while he prospected the local area for the exact spot most favorable for his enterprise. After prodigious toil the party reached Ste. Genevieve only to learn that the village had no building with sufficient capacity to store his goods, and the tired boatmen were forced to push on some ten miles to

Fort Chartres on the east bank, where the basement of the fort was tendered Laclede by the commandant, Neyon de Villiers.

By this time—early November, 1763—word had come to Fort Chartres that it was to be surrendered to the British, and so with his goods safely stored, Laclede proceeded with his step-son, Auguste Chouteau, and a few men to examine the lay of the land at the mouth of the Missouri. Since it is known that Laclede had a knowledge of civil engineering and that he understood the moods of the river, it is not difficult to follow his thoughts as he examined the terrain. He probably would have preferred a location at the confluence of the Mississippi and the Missouri, but at that point the left bank of the Missouri is low, and Laclede would have realized at once that it would be subject to flooding. On the right bank high limestone bluffs rose abruptly from the water's edge, leaving no space for a settlement.

With some regret, no doubt, Laclede retraced his steps some twenty miles to a point where a small stream, later to be known as Mill Creek, entered the Mississippi. Here were low receding limestone bluffs, so that dwellers would need only to utilize this slope to attain safety from any flood; there was a plentiful supply of timber for building and fuel; a large spring ran from a crevice in the limestone; and not least in the favorable features of this site, beyond the crest of the bluffs for a considerable distance there was clear open prairie which would serve as common fields without the labor of clearing. There could be no argument; this site offered all that he was seeking.

Marking the location, the party floated down to the shelter of Fort Chartres to spend the inclement months of December and January, but in February a working crew returned and the construction of quarters was begun. In the spring the families of the men and the trade goods were brought up and the new establishment was ready for business. It was given the name "St. Louis."

The slow growth of the village during its first forty years has been the subject of much discussion. It received additions of population through the abandonment of the French settlements in Illinois in 1764, and its people were reasonably prosperous and apparently happy. Laclede did not die until 1778, fourteen years later, and he was capably succeeded by Auguste Chouteau. Disturbed conditions in Europe probably discouraged emigration and the frequent changes in sovereignty of the Louisiana Territory did nothing to attract colonists.

It has become the practice of modern writers to assume that Laclede foresaw a busy and populous future for his village, and that he was disappointed because it failed to grow more rapidly. There is equal ground, however, for the assumption that he wanted only a place where his business could be conducted with the least interference. Certainly most of his villagers were interested principally in having a comfortable place to live, in exchange for the least labor expended.

Support for the latter theory may be gained from consideration of Ste. Genevieve, the French settlement in Missouri, in which Laclede first stopped. For over two hundred years it has maintained a comfortable and happy existence. Largely uninvaded by "outsiders," its population is less than 3,000 and its citizens are not envious of St. Louis' size and bustle.

When Capt. Amos Stoddard came in 1804 to take possession of the territory in the name of the United States, St. Louis' population, including 268 slaves, was only about a thousand. The community had lived a peaceful existence through the American Revolution and through the period when the young republic was organizing its government. The same officials had administered the law in St. Louis, whether French or Spanish.

The village had been unconcerned as well with the arguments and clashes which had preceded Jefferson's negotiations to acquire the Port of New Orleans, which led to one of the greatest land bargains in history, the purchase of almost half a continent at less than three cents an acre.

The placid quality of the first forty years of St. Louis' history was not destined to persist. Although during the next forty years its population increased only to 16,000, many times that number passed through. Throughout the states on the eastern seaboard, restlessness marked the period which followed the Revolution. The attitude was as if the people had expected that the change of status from crown colonies to free republic would serve to suspend natural laws. Disillusionment seemed to accompany the discovery that if a man lacked wealth, he must still support himself by the sweat of his brow.

Glowing reports came back from friends who had crossed the Alleghenies. In the west, fertile land could be bought at bargain prices. The services of skilled artisans were in demand. It was easy for factory worker or tenant farmer to convince himself that his prospects would be better in the new country.

Driven by the urge for independence, thousands upon thousands of settlers came down the Ohio and up the Mississippi to spread over the west. The village of St. Louis served as the last base of supply before the plunge into the wilderness.

As a part of the nature of the movement, few of the new arrivals possessed sufficient capital to sustain the development of the new communities. The newcomers brought boundless ambition, great energy and enthusiasm, but they lacked money. Furthermore, there was no accumulation of savings in the new country from which to borrow.

Local commerce was conducted largely on a barter basis. Some cash came in through the sale of merchandise in New Orleans and Santa Fe, some through the pay of soldiers, some through the purchase by the Government of supplies which were furnished the Indians. But land purchased from the Government must be paid for in cash, and the surplus was sent to Washington. Since the great desire of most of the people was to buy land, cash was constantly drained away. There was never enough money.

In 1809 St. Louis was incorporated as a town. In 1821, after one of the most bitter fights Congress had experienced, Missouri was admitted as a state. It was the twenty-fourth star in the blue field—the half-way mark in one respect—and the first state located wholly west of the Mississippi River. St. Louis had had two banks. After a career of about two years, each had closed when its assets had become frozen in loans on land. Missouri's first legislature considered at once the question of banking. A state bank was proposed and the proposal defeated. The people did not understand banking and were suspicious of banks. The Legislature tried the experiment of a "loan office," a plan under which the state issued certificates designed to circulate as currency, in denominations of 50c to $10.00, on real estate security, with a limit of $1,000 to one borrower. Before it had been widely used, however, the courts decided that the state had no power to issue currency and the plan was abandoned.

In 1829, in response to earnest and repeated applications, the Bank of the United States opened a branch in St. Louis under the management of Col. John O'Fallon and during its short career it supplied a much needed service. In 1834, however, the charter of the parent bank expired and President Andrew Jackson vetoed the bill renewing it. With the parent out of business, the branch was obliged to close. Since the Federal Treasury was left without a fiscal agent in the west, an arrangement was made with the Commercial Bank of Cincinnati to act as Treasury agent in Illinois and Missouri and that bank opened a branch office in St. Louis in 1835. Although useful and popular at first, the new office soon became an object of suspicion and jealousy and, following the establishment of the Bank of the State of Missouri, it was closed.

The Bank of the State of Missouri opened for business on May 10, 1837. The mistakes of the past, both local and national, had been considered in connection with the preparation of its charter, with beneficial results. Further fortification of the bank's position was provided in its virtual monopoly of the banking field for twenty years, and until after the sale of the state's stock in 1866, the bank's operations remained creditable, both to its sponsors and to its managers.

The weakness of the State Bank was in the lack of vision of its creators, but they are scarcely to be blamed for not foreseeing the increase in volume of business in Missouri over the next twenty years. The Legislature was unwilling to charter private banking, and it hesitated to set up a state bank of sufficient size to care for the needs of the people for fear that such a bank would become too powerful. As a result of this uncertainty, the State Bank was inadequate for its job when it was established, and through the following twenty years, while doing the best it could, it was able to supply only a smaller and smaller part of the demand for banking service.

This lack of facilities led to the establishment by individuals and partnerships of private banking houses. At various times in this period probably twenty to twenty-five firms operated on a large scale. Even an approximation of their volume of business is impossible since, operating without benefit of law, they made no public reports. It is well known that they played an important part in the early development of the state and that they flourished long after the establishment of the State Bank.

St. Louis had a number of newspapers, and in the late 1840s there was a standard make-up of four pages of eight columns each, the pages being larger than those of the present day. Pages one and four were devoted principally to advertising, with editorials and news matter on the inside pages. The editorials were largely partisan political. The news was international, national and local, but was not of the "personal local" type which characterizes modern small town papers. Few illustrations accompanied the news, but the use of small cuts in the classified advertising was frequent. The Mexican War was the main news topic of its day, the principal papers carrying from one-half column to two columns daily, although the news was from one to three months old when published.

There is evidence in the advertisements of the day that St. Louisans need be neither hungry, thirsty, nor bare. The offerings of merchants on a typical day in 1847 included rice, flour, coffee and tea, corn, beans, potatoes, onions, cheese, codfish, mackerel, whiting, sugar, salt, vinegar, butter, pepper, spices, molasses, honey, pickles, raisins, cranberries, dried peaches, dates, pineapples, tomatoes, and ketchup; and so that one need not choke in consuming these items, there were champagne, brandy, Madeira wines, Scotch, Irish, and raw whiskies. "Segars" and tobacco were also available.

There was a wide variety of clothing and fabrics: suits, overcoats, bucksin shirts and drawers, shaker flannel shirts, "gent's" heavy silk undershirts, socks, thick boots, blankets, fancy vestings, handkerchiefs, and both silk and satin cravats. There were India rubber shoes for ladies, shawls, velvet, silk, satinet, feathers, cassimere, alpaca, flannel, oxford, prints, jeans, osnaburg, and drab cloth.

The housewares section, while not as prolific as today, offered brooms, buckets, soap, candles, pins, and Lucifer matches. In heavier goods there were safes, castings, mill stones, nails, white lead, linseed oil, glass, paper, Lehigh coal, logwood, copperas, tar, rope, gunny bags, manila cordage, sail twine, cotton yarn, and hops. Not to be overlooked were theatres, concerts, dancing and music teachers, lotteries, insurance agents, and auctioneers. Subscription to the paper was $8.00 a year. An advertisement of not more than eight lines cost 50c for one insertion, but if the copy stood unchanged, it could run a month for $3.00, a year for $12.00.

On August 2, 1817, there had occurred an event of great significance, but of which little notice was taken at the time. A steamboat of 31.76 tons capacity, the *Zebulon M. Pike*, landed at the foot of Market Street. She was the sixth of eight river steamers to be built that year at Henderson, Kentucky. With a one-story cabin on the main deck and no housing over her wheels, she embodied little prophecy of the magnificence which was to follow, but she was the first steamboat to ply the Mississippi above the mouth of the Ohio and the first to land at St. Louis. Her trip from Louisville, of perhaps five hundred miles, three-fourths of it downstream, had taken six weeks. On July 4, 1870, the *Robert E. Lee* would land at St. Louis, three days, eighteen hours, fourteen minutes out of New Orleans, 1200 miles, all against the current.

From April to October each year St. Louis would see steamboats lined at the levee for over a mile! It would become a port of registration of steam tonnage exceeded only by New York and New Orleans. There would be passenger accommodations not duplicated in the finest hotels in the country. Thousands of tons of shipping would be built in St. Louis boatyards, and more thousands of men would be employed in this industry.

In the second forty years, Laclede's village had grown in population, it was much busier, more cosmopolitan, but its streets were mud, it had no railroad, no telegraph, no water or sewerage system. When it had started to grow, growth had come too rapidly to permit balancing. The physical problems had been so pressing that few persons had found the time to do more than maintain themselves in the swirling current. St. Louis needed men who could give purposeful thought to the welfare of its less fortunate citizens.

THE RECORD-MAKING "ROBT. E. LEE." Although the "Lee" established the New Orleans-St. Louis record, she was built for work, not racing. The banner on the fore-deck, referring to the bales of cotton on board, says "5,741 ROOM FOR MORE".

II

Boatyard Scene

AMONG the passengers landing from a steamboat in 1835, there was a young man who observed with intense interest the stacks of merchandise of endless variety piled on the St. Louis levee. The chanting of the deckhands, the shouting of the draymen, mingled with the noises of steamboat whistles and bells, and the grinding of wheels on cobblestones, were most pleasing to him. George Knight Budd was looking for a place to enter business.

Born in Philadelphia, February 12, 1802, the son of George and Susanah Britton Budd, both members of prominent families, young George Budd had shipped to South American and Mediterranean ports as supercargo on the ships of Henry Pratt. Before coming to St. Louis he had examined the prospects of Cincinnati and of Louisville. The appearance of none of the three towns would have been impressive to a man who had traveled widely, but Budd, in that first glance at the St. Louis waterfront, saw what he wanted. As a matter of statistics, 121 different steamers docked here in 1835, making 803 entries.

Budd did not come empty-handed. Possessing both substantial fortune and broad vision, he was also endowed with a deep sense of social and civic responsibility. After spending his first few years in St. Louis as a merchant, he joined with Andrew Park to form the private banking firm of Budd, Park & Co. which was to remain his principal business interest. He joined and for the rest of his life was an active member of the First Presbyterian Church. He served without pay as the first superintendent of the city schools and as president of the new city board of water commissioners. He was elected city councilman in 1846 and was appointed City Comptroller under Mayor Luther M. Kennett in 1850. As Comptroller, Budd arranged the purchase of a tract of land at Twelfth and Market Streets for use as a park. To most of the citizens the purchase seemed wild extravagance, and their criticism became so severe that Budd was forced to resign. The tract, which is the present location of the City Hall and other municipal buildings, later proved to be one of the greatest bargains the city ever acquired.

In addition to his other activities, Budd found time to serve as agent for Jay Cooke and Company in the sale of United States Bonds during the Civil War, and as financial editor of the *Missouri Democrat*. He was the agent of several large insurance companies and during his latter years he served as president of the Real Estate Savings Institution.

Budd's coming to St. Louis had more or less coincided with the acceleration of the city's growth. From 1800 to 1830 its population had increased from about 1,000 to 6,700. By 1840 it had more than doubled at 16,469. Five years later it had again doubled at 36,265. It would double again by 1850. In 1846 city property was assessed at over $15,000,000. While most citizens looked complacently at the things which had been accomplished, Budd's thoughts turned constantly toward the things which had not been done.

He saw the rapidly increasing mass of undisciplined population living easily, wasting its substance. From his experience as

GEORGE KNIGHT BUDD

Trustee and Director, 1847–1873

a private banker he knew that the Bank of the State of Missouri and the private banks were unable to care for the needs of the community, with the result that the middle and lower classes had practically no banking facilities. He had seen in Philadelphia the successful operation of mutual savings banks and he knew what might be done with them. He knew that although most of the members of the Legislature still favored a monopoly of chartered banking for the State Bank, some legislators realized that this policy was not only unnecessarily restrictive but harmful to the state's progress. He knew that before long a day would come when a charter might be obtained for a bank which would take care of the business not wanted by the existing institutions. He began to talk to his friends about it.

In the beginning only one man, A. B. Chambers, co-publisher with George Knapp of the *Missouri Republican*, was openly enthusiastic. Until his death Chambers remained an aggressive and loyal supporter of the bank. Others approached by Budd, thought of reasons why his plan would not work. The Legislature would protect the State Bank . . . no money could be made from little business . . . no one had the time to take on more activities, even those vitally necessary.

Budd patiently explained his ideas and wore down the objections. This would not be a commercial bank. It would not be a competitor of the State Bank, simply a place where small people could deposit a few dollars safely and earn a little interest— and it might have funds from time to time which could be deposited in the State Bank. The objective was not to make a profit from the operation—he would give all profits to the depositors. Since it was not to be a commercial bank, its surplus would be invested in bonds and real estate loans. That type of banking would require less supervision than a commercial bank. Operation would really be quite simple.

The benefit would come from two sources, Budd patiently pointed out. A happy man was a thrifty man. If the employees of the business houses of the city could be induced to save their money instead of drinking and gambling it away, they would be better workmen. Fewer collections would be necessary for welfare and charity funds. Furthermore, funds being deposited in savings banks in the east, although in "dribs and drabs," aggregated surprisingly large totals and one thing St. Louis still needed almost as badly as anything was investment money.

Doubters, to the number of fourteen, became one by one, at least passive supporters and on February 6, 1847, State Senator William M. Campbell of St. Louis County introduced a bill in the Legislature which would incorporate George K. Budd and fourteen associates, and such others as should be elected by them, as "a body, corporate and politic, by the name of the 'Boatmen's Saving Institution'. . . ."

Budd had been diligent, patient, and discerning in the selection of these men whose names would go before the Legislature as the Trustees of the new Institution. Subsequent events indicate that some of them were permitting the use of their names only for such prestige as they might add toward securing the charter. Since the Legislature had declined so many petitions for banking charters during the previous ten years, Budd had done well to choose carefully.

The original Trustees were:

BASIL W. ALEXANDER, owner of a livery stable, politically influential;
THOMAS ANDREWS, of Andrews and Beakey, Tin, Copper and Sheet Iron Workers, mostly on steamboats;

HENRY D. BACON, son-in-law and partner of Daniel D. Page, considered below;

JAMES G. BARRY, listed in the 1847 directory as a chandler, was City Auditor in 1848, Mayor in 1849;

SULLIVAN BLOOD, Harbor Master, who will be considered in more detail later;

GEORGE K. BUDD, prime mover and early guiding spirit of the Institution;

SAMUEL C. DAVIS, of Davis, Tilden and Richards, wholesale and retail dry goods merchants;

EDWARD DOBYNS, Receiver for the United States Land Office;

LUTHER M. KENNETT, Mayor for three terms from 1850 to 1853, later served in Congress, had earlier been an associate of merchant J. M. White, for whom one of the most famous steamboats on the river was named;

ADAM L. MILLS, who was born before the close of the Revolutionary War, had fought in the battle of Tippecanoe, had been a city councilman and at this time had a contract for the only eastern mail line, running from St. Louis to Louisville. Actual operation of the mail line was handled by others and the fact that Mills was semi-retired doubtless led to his election as first president of the bank;

DANIEL D. PAGE, dealer in real estate, as second Mayor of St. Louis served four one-year terms, partner in the private banking house of Page and Bacon;

LAURASON RIGGS, a member of Riggs & Levering, wholesale grocers;

GEORGE W. SPARHAWK, had been a river pilot, had owned and operated his own boats, had been Harbor Master, and presently was an inspector of steamboats;

AMEDEE VALLE, who had been born in Ste. Genevieve, was an Alderman, a member of the Legislature, at various times dealt in furs, wine, real estate;

JOHN M. WIMER, a Virginian and a blacksmith by trade, was one of the most colorful figures associated with the bank. Political boss of the old Fifth Ward, he was at various times constable, alderman, superintendent of waterworks, postmaster, county judge, sheriff, Mayor (two terms, 1843 and 1857), and member of Congress. As a southern sympathizer during the Civil War he was confined in jail at Alton, Illinois, from which he escaped to join McDonald's forces. He was killed at the battle of Pea Ridge on March 7, 1862. He was so popular in St. Louis that Union authorities would not permit a public funeral for fear it would touch off a riot.

The prestige of Mr. Budd and his associates obtained prompt consideration for the bill[1] and it was approved and signed by Governor John C. Edwards on February 16, just two weeks after the battle of Buena Vista. (Missourians did not yet know the result of the battle, or indeed that it had been fought.) Although its first hurdle was cleared, more than eight months passed before the Bank opened.

Two weeks after the charter was granted, Mr. Chambers, through the columns of the *Missouri Republican*, began to urge the newly elected Trustees to act. No delay, he wrote, should be suffered to put the bank in operation; but another five weeks elapsed before a meeting was called. Then too few Trustees attended to make a quorum. The meeting adjourned and when it was reassembled, only two Trustees appeared. The next day the *Republican* bitterly assailed the Trustees' indifference.

The delay probably was not due entirely to neglect. Budd had his charter, but he had now to get a Board which was willing to go through the tedious work of organization. Ten of the original members, for one reason or another, would remain with him through the opening. The other five, Alexander, Bacon, Barry, Page, and Riggs, felt that they had performed their function and wanted to be relieved of further responsibility.

They were replaced by:

A. B. CHAMBERS, joint owner and editor of the *Missouri Republican*, until his death one of the staunchest supporters of the Bank;

[1]The Act is reproduced in Appendix C.

ADAM L. MILLS
President 1847–1854

JOHN F. DARBY, attorney, one-time Mayor, Congressman, and partner in Darby & Barksdale, a private banking firm;

ALBAN H. GLASBY, member of Gaty, McCune & Glasby, iron founders and steamboat owners;

EDWARD HAREN, a notary;

ASA WILGUS, a painting contractor, specializing on steamboats.

On August 30, eight of the fifteen Trustees met at the *Republican* office and accepted the charter. Another meeting on September 2 saw the adoption of a set of by-laws. These were to be revised, however, before the bank was opened. Other preliminary arrangements had consideration in these meetings. Since there was no capital, nor funds of any sort until deposits should be received, the Trustees agreed each to deposit $25 to provide money for the purchase of supplies.

The report of the Select Committee composed of Wilgus, Budd and Blood, appointed for the purpose of securing quarters for the bank, was made by Mr. Budd at the meeting held on September 20. He said that "the committee had found two places which could be obtained, viz., House on Main Street over Mr. Burtis' Saddlers Shop.[1] Rent $350 per annum. House on Locust Street now occupied by Mr. Cohen.[2] Bonus $400. Rent $150 per annum." Mr. Glasby asked leave to amend the report by adding "the room on North Main Street in the rear of Messrs. Vandeventers' Clothing Store,[3] rent $7 per month." The report was tabled.

Also at the meeting of September 20, Adam L. Mills was elected President and Robert Simpson, Treasurer. There were applications from four men, John D. Taylor, William A. Nelson, James C. Way, and Benjamin B. Chamberlain, for appoint-

[1]Burtis, Joseph K., Saddlery, Hardware, 107 North Main—1847 St. Louis Directory.
[2]Cohen, Albert B., Watchmaker and Jeweler, 16 Locust Street—Ibid.
[3]Vandeventer, J. & W., Clothiers, 162 North Main Street—Ibid.

ment as Secretary. Before balloting, the names of two more, John F. Hunt and Thomas O'. Duncan, were proposed. Mr. Chamberlain received a majority and was declared duly elected.

Simpson had been an army surgeon, operator of the city's first drugstore, postmaster, city collector, member of the Legislature, and was in 1847 City Comptroller. Chamberlain was an auctioneer and commission merchant.

On September 28 Mr. Budd reported that the committee on quarters had engaged the room on Main Street from the Messrs. Vandeventer, but that subsequently Mr. Cohen had offered his lease at $200 instead of $400, and the committee had obtained a release from the Messrs. Vandeventer and had accepted Mr. Cohen's amended offer. The lease on No. 16 Locust Street had approximately two years to run. The committee was instructed to prepare the quarters for occupancy as speedily as possible. The Secretary reported the purchase of "stationary, books, and supplies at a cost of $62.95/100." Committees were appointed to obtain a design for a seal and to prepare an "address for the Public at the opening of the Institution." Perhaps lethargy had marked the action of the Trustees in the spring, but things were humming now.

At a meeting on October 14 it was decided to open for business on Monday, October 18. At the final preliminary meeting on the evening of October 16 Treasurer Simpson's bond in the amount of $10,000, with Edward Bates, Marshall Brotherton and Archibald Gamble as "securities," was approved, as was that of Secretary Chamberlain amounting to $5,000, with Adam L. Mills and Asa Wilgus as "securities."

In March the *Republican* had had a great deal to say about the Trustees' lack of interest in their new responsibilities, but certainly no complaint could have been lodged against their conduct in September and October. In a space of eighteen days they had held ten meetings, and these had been working meetings. Numerous details had been discussed, the by-laws had been written, completely rewritten once, and then amended in six instances before the bank was opened. Nor were the by-laws finished then. That they constantly sought to adjust theory to the practical problems of operation was a credit to the Trustees and attested their serious attitude toward the Institution.

The by-laws provided among other things that each depositor should be furnished an account book (upon payment of 10¢) in which was printed all of the by-laws referring to deposits; that no Trustee should receive any pay for his services; that 3% interest should be allowed on time deposits; and that on Fridays no deposits should be received from males. The by-laws and rules governing the conduct of the officers are reproduced in Appendix D.

The Trustees' hard work in the autumn of 1847 was also an indication of George Budd's ability to attract men who had the knack of getting things done. Those who had served their purpose when the charter was granted were gone. Others would tire of the thankless work before the next year passed. Two groups remained, however, who for slightly different reasons were deeply interested. They would see the Bank on its way.

III

Launching

If October 18, 1847, dawned bright and fair, there is no note of it in the minute book, nor is there any other entry for that day. The Board had met on Saturday evening the 16th and it met again on Tuesday the 19th. Secretary Chamberlain was free, therefore, throughout the opening day to greet customers and well-wishers. Not so Treasurer Simpson. While the volume of business would not have kept his nose in his books all day, he did have some entries to make.

The first depositors were naturally the Trustees. They had agreed each to deposit $25 to provide a fund for the preliminary expenses of the Institution. The first three, however, did not limit themselves to that minimum. Asa Wilgus, Sullivan Blood, and John F. Darby each deposited $100. The fourth name in the cash book is that of Robert Hutton[1] who had no connection with the management. His deposit was $200. George Budd, Amedee Valle, and Adam Mills deposited $25 each. The President signed a check for $200, payment to Albert Cohen for his lease, and at the close of the day the net balance was $375.

On the second day another Trustee, Luther M. Kennett, deposited $30, and Budd appeared with his second deposit, $2,000. On the same day the *Republican* reported:

> "[The bank] opened for the reception of deposits yesterday morning and the business exceeded the most sanguine hopes of

[1]Hutton, Robert, Bookstore, 79 Chestnut St.—1848 St. Louis Directory

its friends. The number of depositors and the amount of deposits gave evidence that the necessity and the utility of such an institution is properly appreciated by the public, or at least a considerable portion of it."

Elsewhere the same issue contained a letter, signed "M," which stated that the writer understood that although the bank had been open only two days, it had deposits of over $2,500. Editor Chambers and Banker Budd were indeed close friends. On October 20 the Budd deposit of $2,000 was withdrawn.

"Expense Fund" deposits of other Trustees straggled in. One held his deposit to $20. Two made no deposit at all, and left the Board within the first six months. Shoe Merchant Samuel Farrington became a depositor on October 20 and Dr. Cheney Howe on the 21st. Printer William Fowler and Manufacturer Daniel Worthington (patent street sprinkler) followed. William Glasgow deposited $60 "In trust for Fanny a woman of color."

The first woman depositor was Mrs. Eliza Colton ($100, on October 23). Mrs. Colton was one day late. Although the Trustees had set aside Friday for "the female community," October 23 was Saturday. As a matter of fact, St. Louisans paid little attention to the Trustees' attempt at segregation of the sexes. Of the first ten deposits made by women, only three occurred on Friday, and during the first three months a number of deposits were made on that day by men. The first "boatman" to appear at the Bank's deposit window was Francis Peine, a hand on the steamer *Utica*. He came on November 6, with $251.

Although the Bank of the State of Missouri and the numerous private banks had more business than they could handle conveniently, Boatmen's had a very slow start. After a month the deposits had grown to only a little over a thousand dollars. The matter of attracting depositors was being discussed at each Board meeting, however, advertisements were being published, and the newspapers, especially the *Republican*, were most generous in their editorial comment.

By November 20 there were sufficient deposits to enable the committee to make an investment. It bought a $1,000 St. Louis city bond bearing interest at 6%, due November 19, 1867, at 85. Although this was a small beginning, Mr. Budd's prophecy that the accumulation of small savings would provide capital for the community was working out. In addition to providing funds for commerce and industry, there has probably been no time since the beginning when the Bank was not the owner of St. Louis city bonds.

While a reasonably good start had been made, the income of $60 a year from the first investment would not go very far toward paying the year's expenses, and this obvious fact caused some very sober thoughts in the minds of Secretary Chamberlain and Treasurer Simpson. Unlike the Trustees, both were dependent upon their employment for their living. Both had accepted jobs and furnished bonds for their faithful performance without having the amount of their salaries set. It might have been in a gesture of complete co-operation, with perhaps the overtones of a gentle reminder, when in December they addressed a joint letter to the Trustees, offering to forego any salary until the Institution should be upon a profitable basis of operation.

The reaction of the Trustees was prompt, generous and void of practical results. They resolved to recompense Messrs. Chamberlain and Simpson for their services up to April 18,

THE BOATMAN'S SAVING INSTITUTION,

Incorporated by the State Legislature, has gone into operation, and is now prepared to receive deposits at the Office, No. **16** Locust, two doors from Main street.

Interest is allowed on deposits at the rate of three per cent. per annum. Safety is guaranteed by the terms of the Charter and By-Laws, which require that the funds of the Institution shall be loaned only on pledges of productive real estate, or such public stocks as are undoubtedly good.

To make money, is not the object of the institution, there being no stockholders, and the trustees giving their services without compensation. It has been established for the benefit of the industrial classes, to afford them and the community generally, a safe place of deposit for their earnings, where at the same time a small interest will accrue.

The names of the officers and trustees are confidently offered to the public as sufficient guarantee that the institution will be conducted in accordance with the charter and by-laws—and while so managed, the perfect safety of all deposits is well secured, and loss impossible. Of the manifest advantage of depositing small sums, to be increased by future additions and the accumulation of interest, it is scarcely necessary to say anything.

The policy is so universally acknowledged and approved, that there is not a city of importance in the United States without its savings institutions. To the boatmen especially, so exposed by his calling to various casualties and the vicissitudes of climate, an institution of the kind offers the strongest inducements, as he may here deposit in safety the small sums which would otherwise be heedlessly and uselessly expended, to accumulate interest, and be ready for his use in the hour of his need.

The office is open for the reception of deposits every day, from ten o'clock, A. M., to four o'clock, P. M., Sundays and holidays excepted; Fridays, however, being specially set apart for the female community.

On application at the office, copies of the charter and by-laws, and all necessary information, will be given by the Treasurer and Secretary, to those desirous of patronizing the Institution.

A. L. MILLS, *President.*
ROB'T. SIMPSON, *Treasurer.*
B. B. CHAMBERLAIN, *Secretary.*

Trustees:

ADAM L. MILLS,
JOHN M. WIMER,
JOHN F. DARBY,
EDWARD DOBYNS,
SULLIVAN BLOOD,

A. H. GLASBY,
L. M. KENNETT,
AMEDEE VALLE,
ASA WILGUS,
EDWARD HAREN,

GEORGE W. SPARHAWK,
THOMAS ANDREWS,
GEO. K. BUDD,
A. B. CHAMBERS,
S. C. DAVIS.

At their meeting on November 16, 1847 the Trustees approved this "Address to the Public" and ordered 1,000 copies printed.

1848, by dividing between them all of the profits the Institution should make by that time. When the first six months had passed and the operation showed a deficit rather than a profit, the Trustees voted an annual salary of $400 each to the Secretary and the Treasurer.

In April, 1848, Samuel C. Davis, Edward Haren, and George W. Sparhawk resigned as Trustees and were succeeded by Augustus Brewster, Alexander Kayser, and Peter Brooks. The Investment Committee had bought 15 shares of stock of the Bank of the State of Missouri at 84, but by the time it had accumulated 50 shares, the price had advanced to 100. The committee reported, moreover, that there were no St. Louis County bonds in the market and that "short city bonds are selling at a price your committee deems inexpedient to pay at present." In June three real estate loans were made in the aggregate amount of $2,350, and in October the bank bought $3,000 St. Louis County 8% Bonds at 100.

Few lending operations long escape the charge of usury. In the first year the Trustees, concerned about their position on this question, requested an opinion from their legal counsel, Edward Bates. A friend of the bank throughout the period from its beginning to his death, Bates probably kept it out of much litigation, and safely guided it when contention was unavoidable. Even while serving as Attorney-General in the first Lincoln cabinet, he wrote from Washington to counsel the bank in connection with the "Floyd Acceptances." His first formal opinion written for the Trustees is interesting for several reasons, but as to its brevity, it must be remembered that it was written by Bates' own hand with a quill pen. The typewriter, its many benefits admitted, has served to lengthen legal opinions.

"St. Louis, June 14th, 1848

Communication:

A. L. Mills, Esq.

The Boatmen's Saving Institution is authorized to lend money at 6 pr ct interest and you put the question, whether it will make a loan usurious, if you take payment of Interest in advance, which is the same thing as discount. I am of opinion that the time of paying the Interest is immaterial and so is the fund out of which the Debtor pays it.

The books of Report are full of cases declaring, that it is not usurious in Banks to take the Interest on their loans in advance. They call the operation discounting. But discounting is nothing more or less than retaining the amount of Interest out of the sum lent, instead of receiving it out of some other fund belonging to the borrower. I think the Institution may lend its funds in the way proposed, without the fear of usury.

Very respectfully,

Edw. Bates"

The first anniversary was at hand and it was a time to take stock and see what had been accomplished. The "Committee on the State of the Institution" reported that there were 186 depositors (164 Male, 22 Female) and that the total deposits were $26,274.91. Interest received during the year had totaled $862.21. Of this, $303.10 had been credited to depositors on time or savings accounts, leaving net income before expenses $559.11. Expenses were $1,542.45, so that in spite of rigid economy and purely nominal salaries for the Secretary and the Treasurer, there was a deficit of $983.34.

A majority of the Trustees thought that probably the name of the Bank had kept away persons who were not connected with the river trade, and it was resolved to ask the General Assembly to change the name to "St. Louis Saving Institution," but at the next meeting of the Board, upon motion of Mr. Budd, this action was rescinded.

It was also resolved to petition the Assembly to permit the Institution to charge 8 per cent interest on loans, and to make loans on personal notes up to $500, provided there were two endorsers. The latter request was granted, the former declined by the Legislature the next February.

The Trustees felt that if deposits could be brought up to $100,000, the Institution could operate profitably, and a committee was appointed to "memorialize the different Insurance Offices, the Public School Directors, and the Gas Light Company" to deposit their funds in the Institution. The resignation of Peter Brooks, who had served as Trustee only since April, was accepted.

Of the fifteen original Trustees and the eight who had been elected to fill vacancies, nine had resigned by October 18, 1848. The records of the Bank contain no explanation of this large turnover, but the reasons for it can probably be read between the lines. As has already been mentioned, it is probable that the five who resigned before the bank opened did so because they had been willing to help Budd get the Institution started, but from the beginning had not been interested in helping with its operation. The withdrawal of the others, as well as subsequent events, seems to indicate a fundamental difference of opinion in the Board as to the eventual place of the Bank in the community.

Mr. Budd and Mr. Chambers (sometimes Mr. Kennett and others sided with them) were chiefly interested in doing a small banking business without too much thought about making a profit. Others, and probably the majority, were willing at the moment that the Bank should serve small customers, but they wanted the operation to produce a substantial profit. While the Trustees could not share in such profits personally, their pride was involved and they undoubtedly realized that with the element of risk which is inherent in any lending operation, the Bank might suffer losses, and since it had no capital, bank losses would mean a loss to individual depositors. Although the Trustees were under no legal liability, the moral obligation of such an event might be felt very keenly in a small, close-knit community, especially if the loss fell, as it would, upon persons of small means.

Beyond these considerations, these men had the feeling that the monopoly granted the State Bank would not be held forever, and that when the break came, a bank already firmly established and operating would have a definite advantage over those banks which would start at that time. A few of these men were willing to hold on and wait for that opportunity, while others grew impatient and resigned their trusteeships. They respected and liked Budd, but there are indications that they thought many of his ideas impractical. The first open evidence of this was not to come until the election of the second president of the Bank in 1854.

At the meeting on November 7, 1848, Joseph Throckmorton, a popular steamboat operator, was elected Trustee to succeed Peter Brooks. In January, 1849, Alexander Kayser resigned and was replaced by Robert Holmes. In April of the same year the salaries of the Secretary and the Treasurer were raised to $600 per annum and the first loan was made on personal security, $500 to Isaac W. Taylor, an attorney, upon the endorsement of E. K. Mason, his law partner, and John Stacker.

The year 1849 was one of misfortune for St. Louis. Through the spring and summer a cholera epidemic raged. In July alone there were over 600 deaths from cholera. As if this were not enough disaster to be visited upon one community, on May 17 the steamer *White Cloud* caught fire. The flames spread to the *Eudora* and the *Edward Bates*. When the *Bates'* hawsers burned through, the flaming craft drifted downstream, setting fire to the mile-long string of boats at the wharf. A brisk northeast breeze carried the flames first to the piles of merchandise stacked on the levee and then to the buildings fronting the river.

When the fire was finally stopped, twenty-three steamers and four hundred and thirty buildings had been destroyed. The building in which the Bank was quartered was not seriously damaged, but those on three sides of it had been burned. Main Street, laid out some eighty years before, had long been too narrow for the bustling business it carried, and the city seized upon this opportunity to widen it. The widening left George Collier, who owned the building site on the southwest corner of Main and Locust Streets, as well as the bank building directly west of it, too little ground on which to reconstruct his main building without tearing down the latter, and he gave notice to the Bank that he would not extend its lease.

Rooms were obtained in a building at 52 North Second St. (on the west side, just south of Pine St.) owned by Peter D. Papin, at a yearly rental of $300. An appropriation of $50 provided for signs, painting, counters, and refurbishing. Neither at the meeting called for October 16 nor for October 23 was there a quorum, a very unusual occurrence, but on October 30 the usual procedure of an annual meeting was carried out.

The minutes recorded that during the second year deposits had increased from $26,274.91 to $49,527.96, depositors from 186 to 250. Of the 64 new depositors, 53 were males, 11 females. Although the result for the second year was scarcely as creditable as that for the first, no comment and no plans were recorded. Undoubtedly the poor showing was due largely to the severe epidemic and the devastating fire, and the Trustees counted themselves fortunate to maintain their ground. The salary of the Secretary was increased to $800 a year, but in April, 1850, Mr. Chamberlain resigned and shortly thereafter died. Edward Dobyns resigned as Trustee and was succeeded by Hudson E. Bridge, an iron founder, manufacturer of stoves and plows, and man of many affairs.

The new Secretary was Joseph W. Thornton, who would cause the Trustees many worries. It is possible that wishes have been expressed that other officers of Boatmen's, and perhaps other banks, should be hanged, but as far as is known, Thornton is the only one who achieved this end. The Trustees were destined to regret his election.

At the third annual meeting on October 18, 1850, the Treasurer's report showed $41,729.12 in bonds, stocks, deeds of trust, and accrued interest, but no report was entered of the total deposits, the number of depositors, nor the cash on hand. Again there were no proposals for improvement of the Bank's business, but in December another petition to the Legislature was prepared, asking relief from the restrictions on real estate loans; reduction of the number of Trustees from 15 to 11, with five as a quorum; permission to charge 8% interest, "as the Institution would thereby be enabled to allow 5% to depositors . . ."

THE ST. LOUIS LEVEE, 1850. There was still no railroad, and all heavy traffic moved by water. Each year from April to November steamboats lined the levee.

In February the Legislature granted all of these requests. The foot which had been inserted in the crack of the door in 1847 had now been able, after four years, to widen that crack— a little. Messrs. Brewster, Darby, and Throckmorton resigned to reduce the number of Trustees to eleven. The meeting of March 20, 1851, at which these resignations were accepted was the last one recorded in the original minute book, and a new one was opened with the meeting of April 18.

As if turning a new minute-book leaf were attended by magic, the Bank began to show profits. Although its money had gone begging at 6%, twenty-one personal notes were offered on May 14 for discount at 8%. The State Bank had passed its dividend and undoubtedly had tightened on its lending, which probably accounted for the increased activity at Boatmen's. The Trustees were considering how they might dispose of their stock in the State Bank.

The Bank awoke from its dullest period to one of seething activity. In the spring of 1851 the Board issued instructions to President Mills, which must have kept that venerable man extremely busy. In addition to his efforts to sell the fifty shares of stock of the Bank of the State of Missouri at no less than cost, he had to try to find a more suitable building. In the Papin house the Bank was bulging at the seams. There were so many applications for loans that the Board agreed that it was no longer practical for the Secretary to list detail in the minutes. From this point on there was recorded simply the total amount offered, accepted, or rejected.

In July the President was authorized to lease rooms in the *Missouri Republican* Building at No. 9 Chestnut Street for five years at an annual rental of $500. Contemporary publications carry pictures of the *Republican* building in which the Bank's quarters are plainly marked, and this is the first location of which an authentic illustration is available. In the Bank's Fiftieth Anniversary Booklet there are illustrations of the type commonly termed "artist's conceptions" of the first two buildings. It is possible that in 1897 someone remembered their appearance and that the drawings are accurate. Since neither building remained standing at that time, however, their authenticity must be questioned.

When it is considered that the $300 rental of the Papin house was not being earned in 1850, the five-year lease at $500 in the new location a year later represented an enormous venture. Also authorized was the expenditure of $300 for a safe purchased from Christopher Rhodes, Esq. That it was a safe opened by a key, and the disposition of its keys, would be featured in an investigation to be held some three years later.

At the annual meeting in October it was recommended that a clerk be employed at a salary of not over $600 a year to assist the Secretary and the Treasurer. At the same time the cautious suggestion was made that the salaries of those two officers not be raised until "the opening of Spring."

The Bank was stepping into a wider field. But it had not left the field of small banking. In December, 1851, for example, the Board approved the application of Capt. Hewitt, of the steamer *Highland Mary No. 2*, to withdraw $59 from the account of his former deckhand, William McKee, deceased. William's money was needed by his family and was to be released, without probate, upon proper indemnification.

Although Boatmen's business was booming, there are indications that other banking houses were not finding such ready use for their money. On December 31, 1851, Boatmen's declined a deposit of $100,000 by Messrs. E. W. Clark & Bros. and the next week passed a resolution that interest stop on any account when the balance exceeded $15,000, unless some special arrangement be made. When the Bank had excess funds, they were being divided approximately evenly between Page & Bacon, L. A. Benoist & Co., and Loker, Renick & Co.

The suggestion for the employment of a clerk had not been carried out, but by March 11 applications were on file from C. V. Harris, Alfred Tracey, Barrett Williams, R. Mackwitz, Samuel C. Gaylord, T. J. Montgomery, and from W. B. Finch in behalf of his son. Gaylord received the appointment. In July Messrs. Lucas & Simonds were added to the list of depositories and, after discussion at three meetings, the application of Francis Beehler for a $12,000 real estate loan—the largest yet to be considered—was finally declined. The rejection of the Beehler loan was undoubtedly occasioned by its size and character since in August the Board approved a real estate loan of $2,000 to Dr. William Beaumont, a name famous in St. Louis medical annals.

No particular notice was accorded the fifth anniversary. Reflecting the increased activity of the past eighteen months, the salaries of the Secretary and the Treasurer were raised to $1,000 a year and that of the newly appointed clerk to $700. The State Bank stock remained unsold and the President was authorized to sell it at par without back dividends. Unfavorable conditions in the State Bank were giving Boatmen's wide opportunities and the Trustees were anxious to make the most of them.

Accordingly the Board decided to petition the Legislature for still broader powers and in February, 1853, these were granted. The changes thus made in the charter raised the loan limit, on personal security, from $500 to $2,500 and permitted the issuance of negotiable certificates of deposit in denominations of not less than $100. The Legislature did not intend that Boatmen's should become a bank of issue for small currency.

In February, after a trial to see if his handwriting should be satisfactory, Harry Boggs was employed as assistant bookkeeper at $1,000 per year and Charles S. Blood, the son of Sullivan Blood, was employed as a clerk at $400 per year. This action increased the number of employees to five. The demand for loans was so active that the Treasurer was authorized to sell some of the holdings of bonds in order to provide more funds for lending. Remaining suspicion of the State Bank was reflected in a resolution adopted in March instructing the officers not to accept after banking hours any checks drawn on the Bank of the State of Missouri in payment of loans. In April Thomas Andrews, one of the original Trustees, resigned and was replaced by William D'Oench, an importer and wholesaler of drugs and chemicals.

It had been the practice up to this time to consider discounts only once a week. Pressure of business by June, 1853, forced the Board to designate two discount days each week, Tuesday and Friday. In September, as if the Trustees might have had some premonition of an approaching event indicated in a previous paragraph, the officers were instructed to employ a "night guard" and "to make such alterations in the fastenings, bars and other protections of the office as they may deem necessary."

It will be recalled that the minutes of the third and fourth annual meetings contained no full report of the condition of the

Bank, as if the Trustees were anxious to overlook what to them must have been an unhappy state of affairs. Although conditions had improved considerably by the time of the fifth anniversary, again no special notice had been taken of the status of the business. The sixth annual statement, however, entered in full, showed deposits of $372,215.57 and loans and investments over $300,000. There was a surplus in the value of assets over deposits of $8,823.45. Deposits had shown an increase of over $100,000 since April, a remarkable gain for the six-month period. There were 857 depositors, 74 of whom were females. The committee's report included the statement, "Not a dollar has been lost by bad debts, only one note being under protest or in suit and that is fully secured and the money will be made."

Then, as if they were a little ashamed of the austerity of their quarters in the midst of such prosperity, the Trustees instructed the Secretary to purchase a carpet for the discount room at a cost not to exceed 75c a yard. In December the committee which had been appointed to consider the propriety of receiving the deposit of city funds reported adversely. Although no reason was given, the fact that it would have been necessary to secure these funds probably made their use seem impractical to the Trustees.

As indicated by the events just recorded, the Bank entered the year 1854 with the fairest prospects since its opening, but its tranquil progress was not to continue long. On the morning of April 6 when Mr. Simpson entered the Bank with the negro George who built fires, the door of the safe was wide open! A hurried checkup revealed that over $19,000 had been stolen, $1,595 in gold and the rest in notes of Missouri banks. The

Trustees were immediately summoned to a special meeting at which they questioned all employees. This investigation revealed that the money had been taken from the large safe (the Rhodes safe), the keys to which had been kept in the small safe, and that it had been the practice to hide a key to the small safe somewhere about the premises at night, usually in the chandelier.

Only one statement was made which might have furnished any clue. Secretary Thornton testified that the key which was usually hidden in the chandelier was frequently not removed from its hiding place until after customers had entered the Bank in the morning and that many people might have had a chance to learn of its secret location. No other employee made any statement which might have been interpreted as an attempt to turn suspicion toward outsiders. The Board instructed the President to offer a reward of $1,000 for the arrest and conviction of the robber and a reward of $4,000 for the return of the money. Although the Trustees did not announce publicly that deposits were impaired over $8,000, they did publish their guarantee that depositors would suffer no loss. The reward went begging, and none of the money was ever recovered by the Bank, although most of it would again rest in its safe.

Offers of assistance from the Bank of the State of Missouri and several private banking houses were declined with thanks and, as it turned out, such help was not needed since no public excitement resulted from the robbery, the depositors apparently relying on the guarantee of the Trustees. It is doubtful, of course, if many people realized the seriousness of the situation. In six and one-half years of operation the Bank had accumulated a surplus over liabilities of about $11,000 and this, together with $8,000 more, had been stolen. A record of the investigation was carefully kept, but was not entered in the minute book until January, 1856, when the old charter had been surrendered. The notation preceding the entry states that "these records have been preserved by the President and for 'prudential reasons' not heretofore entered."

On May 24 the death of A. B. Chambers was announced to the Board and there could be no doubt that the resolution of regret which was adopted was fully sincere. He had been one of the strongest supporters of the Institution from the first time the matter was discussed with him by Mr. Budd.

On June 14, 1854, a series of significant changes determined upon by the Trustees began. The resignation of Adam Mills as President came before the Board. On the morning of April 6 he had asked to be excused from the meeting investigating the robbery because he had become suddenly ill. Doubtless he felt very keenly his responsibility for the safe-keeping of the Bank's funds, in which he seemed to have failed. The election of his successor at this meeting brought into clear focus the division in the Board which has been mentioned earlier. On the first three ballots the vote stood: Blood five, Budd one, Wilgus one. On the fourth ballot Blood received six votes, Asa Wilgus one, and Blood had been elected.

After the third ballot Budd had decided that he would gain no support by holding out, and he cast the deciding vote for Blood. The Bank was to prosper by that decision. If Budd was disappointed by his failure to become president, it did not affect his loyalty to the Bank. He continued to serve on the Board throughout Blood's administration, supporting ably the sound policies the President advocated.

Capt. Blood had been born in Windsor, Vermont, in 1795 and had come to Missouri at an early age. Shortly after his arrival he became a member of the St. Louis constabulary and when Lafayette visited the city in 1826, he served as Marshall of the Day. He had entered the steamboat trade and had been the master and owner of several steamers. A man of great energy and integrity, his business ability was to be proved in his administration of the Bank's affairs over the next seventeen years.

One more step which was to have a lasting effect upon the career of the Bank was taken at this time. Rufus J. Lackland was elected Trustee to succeed A. B. Chambers. June also brought the resignation of Robert Simpson as Treasurer. Although there was no hint of any personal responsibility on his account for the robbery, he was a very old man and the Board undoubtedly felt that Alton R. Easton who succeeded him, being much younger, would be of greater value to the Institution. In September a by-law was adopted:

> "Any clerk or officer of the Institution who shall be seen manifestly under the effects of alcoholic drink while in the Institution shall forthwith be discharged by the Board on evidence being submitted to them of this fact."

Whether on account of this by-law, or whether occasioned by mounting suspicion of his connection with the robbery, on November 28 Joseph W. Thornton resigned as Secretary. Subsequently he was indicted by the grand jury for the robbery and in 1858 was brought to trial. In the course of the proceedings Joseph Charless, President of the Bank of the State of Missouri, testified that Thornton had come to that bank some time after the robbery with a package of bank notes for redemption. They were covered with mud, were watersoaked,

SULLIVAN BLOOD
President 1854–1871

and appeared to have been buried. Upon being questioned by Mr. Charless, Thornton stated that the notes had been found under a stump by a steamboat deckhand when he had been sent ashore to throw a line over this stump to tie up the boat. The man, he continued, did not know whether the bills had any value and had sold them to Thornton for a trifle. Mr. Charless advised him that since the bills had been found, they should be advertised, whereupon Thornton had taken his package and left.

Samuel Gaylord and other Boatmen's employees testified that after Thornton had left the Bank's employ he had opened an account there, and that their attention had been attracted by its activity. It had been Thornton's practice over a considerable period to deposit a number of bills, one or two of which had obviously been watersoaked. He would then withdraw fresh currency. A few days later this would be redeposited together with one or more notes which showed the effects of having been soaked in water. As this process continued, the tellers had begun to make a note of the serial numbers of the bills which they paid out, and thus were able to check them as they were included in subsequent deposits.

Thornton did not take the stand in his own behalf, but presented several character witnesses who stated that he had always been a man of good reputation. Although the circumstantial evidence was very strong, the defendant was acquitted.

Thornton took deep offense against Mr. Charless on account of his testimony and a year later when they met on Market Street, Thornton drew a pistol and killed Charless. Because of Charless' personal popularity, a mob formed and Thornton's lynching was prevented only by prompt and aggressive action by the sheriff. In due course he was tried for the murder, convicted, and hanged by the neck until dead.

Returning to the Bank's events of the year 1854, although local conditions had been very favorable, an impending national monetary disturbance clouded the horizon. The storm struck St. Louis early in 1855. Page & Bacon had been financing the construction of the Ohio & Mississippi River Railroad. Toward the end of 1854 the banking house was experiencing difficulty in selling enough of the road's bonds to meet construction accounts. Consequently Henry Bacon made a trip to New York where he was promised assistance by the banking firm of Duncan, Sherman & Co. Much elated, Bacon returned to St. Louis in January, only to find a message that Duncan, Sherman & Co. had withdrawn their commitment. Page & Bacon were forced to suspend, and after reopening for a short time later in the year, the firm was closed permanently. Its suspension started a run on other financial institutions and on Saturday, January 13, Boatmen's paid out approximately $100,000, or almost one-third of its deposits.

The only recorded meeting of the Board ever held on Sunday occurred on January 14, 1855. The notice for the meeting stated that it was occasioned by "the extraordinary and alarming crisis in the financial institutions of the city, produced by the sudden and unlooked for events of yesterday." After full discussion it was resolved, "That the Boatmen's Saving Institution will continue payments to depositors as long as there is money on hand."

As a result of another meeting which had occurred on that Sunday, however, on Monday morning there appeared in the downtown district handbills carrying a notice "To the Public."

TO THE
PUBLIC!

The undersigned, KNOWING and RELYING on the AMPLE ABILITY of the following Banking Houses, iu the city of St. Louis, and with a view of quieting the public mind in regard to the safety of deposits made with them, hereby pledge themselves and offer as a guarantee, THEIR PROPERTY, to make good all deposits with either of said Banking Houses; to wit:

Messrs. "LUCAS & SIMONDS," "BOGY, MILTENBERGER & Co.," "TESSON & DANJEN," "L. A. BENOIST & CO.," "JNO. J. ANDERSON & CO.," "DARBY & BARKSDALE," and "BOATMEN'S SAVING INSTITUTION."

J. O'Fallon,	Ed. Walsh,
J. B. Brant,	Louis A. Labeaume,
L. M. Kennett,	D. A. January,
John How,	James Harrison,
Andrew Christy,	Charles. P. Chouteau.
Greeley & Gale,	Wayman Crow,
Sam'l B. Wiggins,	R. J. Lockwood,
Switzer, Platt & Co.	Wm. L. Ewing,
R. M. Funkhouser & Co.	Chas. Tillman,
Amedee Berthold,	Isaac Walker.
Greene Erskine,	John C. Rust,

St. Louis, January 15, 1855.   of Firm of Adolphus Meier & Co.

A reproduction of the handbill circulated on
January 15, 1855.

The notice was signed by twenty-two of the most substantial citizens of St. Louis and it guaranteed the deposits of six private banking houses as well as Boatmen's Saving Institution. (The only known original copy of this handbill was preserved in the Bank's records and is reproduced on the opposite page.) This foresighted and generous co-operation stopped the excitement locally and after a short period of stagnation St. Louis' business activity was resumed.

An interesting story in connection with the excitement of Saturday, January 13, 1855, has been brought to the attention of the Bank by the grandson of an eye witness. His grandfather told him that on that afternoon, when long lines of depositors were standing outside the Bank, a carriage drew up at the door and out of it had stepped a handsome and expensively dressed woman carrying a heavy carpetbag. She was well known to most of the observers as the proprietor of the city's most exclusive bordello. She elbowed her way between the lines, saying "You so-and-so's, get out of my way; you're trying to take money out, and I want to put money in this bank." Having made her way inside, someone helped her lift her carpetbag to the counter and when it was opened, out poured $50,000 in gold. The story continues that this was what stopped the run on the bank. While the story is not true in its entirety, the fact is that on that afternoon, the records show, this woman did deposit $4,500 in gold which remained on deposit through most of that year. Not only the prominent men of the city, but many other persons as well were interested in the preservation of the Boatmen's Saving Institution.

The recovery from the panic had been prompt and vigorous and the Bank under Mr. Blood's leadership was attracting more and more business. Showing a profit less than $11,000 in its first six and one-half years of existence, in the eighteen months following the robbery it made $22,000, entirely replacing the loss and providing a small surplus. The time had come, in the opinion of the Trustees, to move toward changing the Institution into an out-and-out commercial bank. Accordingly they applied to the Legislature for a new charter which would permit them to sell stock and to broaden their activities.

Boatmen's first chapter was about to be closed. As the end approached, an incident occurred which carried a note of pathos. In December, 1855, Adam Mills presented a bill to the Board for $2,200 for his services as President. The account stated that his first year's service was gratuitous and he asked $400 per year for the succeeding five and one-half years. He was a man of some fortune and did not need the money. It was the act of a man in his dotage and the Trustees declined to make any payment to him. He died the following February 6.

IV

Shakedown Cruise

THERE is an old saying that a watched pot never boils. Captain Blood and his close associates must have felt keenly the sense of this adage as they waited through the years for Boatmen's pot to boil. They were now at the end of their vigil. Gradually, carefully, they had pressed their case with the Legislature until they had freed themselves from the early restrictions. They had finally brought the original Institution to the point where it was making money, and future prospects were favorable indeed.

The culmination of their years of effort came on November 30, 1855, when the Legislature granted a new charter with a provision for the issuance of capital stock from $100,000 to $500,000, as the Directors[1] might see fit. The new charter gave the power to receive deposits ("from Boatmen, and from others," it read, as had the first charter), to lend money at rates up to 8%, to discount notes, to execute trusts, but not to issue notes for circulation as money. It made provision for the distribution of the profits of the "old institution" among persons who had maintained deposits of $100 or more from April 18, 1848, to the date when the original charter should be surrendered.

The Trustees would have preferred to have the capital greater than $500,000. From past experience, however, they

---

[1] In the new charter the board members were called "Directors" rather than "Trustees."

knew that it would be difficult to induce the Legislature to grant a request for such an amount; and even if acquiescence could be obtained, it was almost sure to be accompanied by unwelcome restrictions.

In their negotiations with the Legislature, therefore, although quite modest in their request for authorized capital, the Trustees managed to insert in the new charter a provision which would permit accumulation of capital funds greater than any amount which that body in 1855 would have been willing to allow them. Under this provision the Directors at each five-year anniversary after January 1, 1856, might review their situation, and if they saw fit, declare a dividend.

If in cash, such dividends were to be limited to one-fourth of the profit for the five-year period. The remainder might be reserved for the benefit of depositors, or might be declared as stock dividends, notwithstanding that this might increase the capital beyond the original authorization.

Under this liberal arrangement the Directors were limited as to capital only by their ability to make profits. No dividend was paid until December 31, 1870, and although capital at that time remained at $400,000, surplus had grown to $2,293,000.

There was further evidence late in 1855 that the Legislature was weakening in its determination to maintain a monopoly for the State Bank. In December it granted charters to several other banking institutions. While all of these were modeled closely upon Boatmen's, none had fewer privileges, and some had more. One of them was permitted to charge rates of interest up to 10%. Another, The St. Louis and Carondelet Savings Institution, was granted "all of the privileges of Boatmen's Saving Institution."

If there had been apathy among Boatmen's Trustees toward the original charter, none was exhibited now. The Directors met on December 13 and accepted the charter, and during the next two weeks they held seven more meetings and were ready to open the "new" institution on January 2.

The new Board included Sullivan Blood, George Budd, Luther Kennett, John Wimer, and Adam Mills, who had been original Trustees; Carlos Greeley, Rufus Lackland, William D'Oench, Louis LaBeaume, Robert Holmes, Asa Wilgus who had been elected later; and Adolphus Meier, a new member. Three Board members attended all eight organization meetings; three attended seven; three, six. Mr. Mills attended only one; he was approaching the end. Budd and Kennett, although they remained on the Board for many years after, attended none of these meetings. The old mutual bank was gone. It had failed to fit its environment; but it had been adapted by hands that were to prove very skillful in shaping the further career of the Bank.

The Directors' acceptance of the charter met with general approval. The newspapers supported the Bank as usual. A letter published in the *Evening News*, however, severely criticized the action. The writer blamed the members of the Board for not paying the robbery loss out of their own pockets, charged them with having spent the Bank's money injudiciously in obtaining the new charter, and ended: "This comes of persons undertaking the management of matters they are not interested in. It will be well for the new stockholders to watch the proceedings." It is a part of Nature's plan that there should be pessimists as well as optimists in order to have a healthy balance of opinion. Perhaps the caution which prompted the writer to send this letter saved him many dollars which might have been lost in speculation; but if he had subscribed for a share of Boatmen's stock at $100 in December, 1855, by September, 1873, he could have realized $775 from the investment.

The Board decided to offer $100,000 of stock and when the subscription book was opened on December 20, that amount was subscribed before noon. Many persons complained that they had not had an opportunity to buy the stock they wanted, and on December 26, $300,000 additional stock was offered and promptly subscribed. The $100,000 of remaining authorized stock was never offered for sale.

For the forty-five "original $100 depositors" three shares each were set aside, since it had been found that the value of the furniture and fixtures, less $29 for "books not used by this institution," were worth $1,798.65. This, added to the accumulated surplus, amounted to $13,500.

One of the original depositors, a steamboat captain, Thomas Dennis, had deposited $100 in 1847, and in 1849 he had gone to California, leaving his account undisturbed. The three shares set aside for him were unclaimed in 1856 and at the time of the subsequent re-capitalization in 1873. On May 5, 1874, however, Dennis' son-in-law, James M. Lane, appeared at the Bank with the original deposit book and credentials as the legal representative of Dennis' heirs, to claim the deposit and the stock. With the accretions in dividends and interest, he received a check for $2,565. The almost forgotten $100 had earned at the rate of just under 100% a year.

Sullivan Blood was elected President, with a salary of $1,200 and Alton R. Easton cashier, salary $2,000. The presidency was still not a full time job. The cashier was instructed to

AT SECOND AND PINE STREETS

*The first of its homes built by Boatmen's, and
occupied by it from 1856 to 1891.*

address James Punnett, Esq., cashier of the Bank of America, New York City, with reference to the deposit of $50,000 in that bank to facilitate dealing in exchange. A committee was appointed to report on securing a perminent (sic) location for the Bank. James Smith, of Partridge & Co., wholesale grocers, was elected to succeed Adam Mills as Director.

In 1852 the Bank had taken an enormous step in increasing its rent from $300 to $500 a year. It now attempted to obtain a twenty-year lease on a building at Main and Chestnut Streets, offering $3,000 a year for the first ten years and $3,500 a year for the second ten. It is indicative of the desirability of property adjacent to the waterfront that the owner declined this offer. The Directors then decided to construct their own building, purchased from "Doct. Hill and others" a lot on the northeast corner of Second and Pine Streets, fronting twenty-two feet on Second and fifty-eight feet deep, for $12,000. They bought also the adjacent property at the rear, fronting eighteen feet on Pine and forty-one feet deep, from Sullivan Blood for $5,500, paying $700 to one of the occupants to vacate. Architects were invited to submit designs in competition and that of Barnett & Weber was accepted, with C. H. Pond being awarded second prize. Zepheniah T. Knott was employed as superintendent of construction. The building was to be of brick, three stories and basement; it would cost about $30,000 and would be occupied by the Bank from January 31, 1857, until March 1, 1891.

The Republican said on February 1, 1857:

> "The new bank is an ornamental building, highly embellishing that portion of Second Street ... It is one of the best built ... in the city ... The general effect of the front room is that of convenience, neatness, and beauty ... [The vaults']

cold steel walls and burglar proof locks will resist all attempts
to cut, bore or pick . . ."

Although the new vaults might be considered perfectly safe,
only a small part of the Bank's surplus funds was kept there,
most being kept on deposit at the private banks because it
would earn interest. When discounts went up, however, balances with the private banks dropped suddenly, and these
banks complained frequently about paying high interest rates
on balances in view of their instability. One controversy with
Lucas & Simonds was settled by an agreement that Boatmen's
would not let its balance there fall below $50,000, provided the
firm paid 6% on all deposits. By custom these funds were
secured with marketable securities or by personal bonds.

In its first statement after the reorganization Boatmen's
showed total assets of more than a million dollars; real estate
loans and investments were only about $35,000, but it had
discounts of over $700,000, exchange about $100,000, and
more than $200,000 cash. Net profits for the first six months of
1856 were $17,000, considerably more than that for the pre-
vious eight years, after the robbery loss had been charged off.
There were 2,227 depositors, but the old practice of reporting
the number of females among these had been discontinued. The
business of the community had increased so greatly that although the State Bank, a number of private banks, and a number of saving institutions were flourishing, St. Louis was still
short of banking capital.

Missouri's first general banking law was enacted by the
Legislature in 1857, following an amendment to the state constitution the year before. This amendment permitted the chartering of new banks of issue, but limited to $20,000,000 the

aggregate capital of the authorized new banks. A rush resulting from this legislation placed before the General Assembly early in 1857 applications for banking charters with an aggregate capital of $43,500,000.

This activity suggested to some of Boatmen's Directors that they should be thinking about protecting their position, and a committee of the Board was appointed to present a report on the matter. The report recommended that the Bank ask (1) for an authorized capital of $1,000,000; (2) for the removal of the restriction preventing one individual from holding more than 100 shares of stock; (3) for the right to pay out annually in dividends 80% of the profits of the preceding year; and (4) for the privilege of issuing notes with denominations as low as $5 to circulate as currency. Nine members of the Board were present at the meeting and the recommendations were adopted by a five to four vote, Messrs. Greeley, LaBeaume, Meier, Smith, and Wimer favoring, and Messrs. Blood, Budd, Lackland, and Wilgus opposing.

Mr. Lackland, as a member of the committee, presented a minority report in which he stated that he differed "in toto" with the conclusion of the other members, and Mr. Budd filed a written protest against the proposed action. While Budd had given up the idea of being able to operate a small banking business, he remained on the conservative side in considering the problems of commercial banking and in this instance he was joined by Blood and Lackland who probably had more practical ideas of banking than any of the other Directors.

The petition was filed with the Legislature, where it naturally became involved with the jumble of banking matters before that body and remained without action during the regular session. At a special session late in 1857 it was passed, but was vetoed by Governor Stewart and was allowed to die. Since the petition was presented to the Legislature, and never withdrawn, it cannot be assumed that the majority of the Board did not approve. In view of the vigorous opposition by Lackland and Budd, and concurrence by Blood and Wilgus, however, it seems unlikely that the requested privileges would have been fully used if they had been granted. The Bank was making money and there were provisions in its charter which would provide sufficient capital without further favor from the Legislature. Captain Blood and Mr. Lackland felt that the Bank would be better off to proceed slowly with the privileges it had.

One provision of the Banking Act of 1857 was that the banks chartered under it should be subject to examination, which was necessary, of course, in order that the conditions under which currency was issued could be controlled. It is likely that the Legislature's insistence upon examination made it much easier for Captain Blood and Mr. Lackland to restrain the other members of the Board from insisting on having a new charter. The State Savings Institution had received one of the new charters under the 1857 Act, but never accepted it, probably on account of the fact that as a bank of issue, it would have been subject to examination. The six new banks to be opened in St. Louis were the Southern, the Merchants, the Mechanics, the Bank of St. Louis, the Exchange, and the City, but only the first four of these were opened in 1857.

The soundness of the restraint enforced on Boatmen's by the minority of its Board was very quickly proved. In August, 1857, the Ohio Life and Trust Company of Cincinnati failed, precipitating a severe financial crisis, the first effects of which were felt in St. Louis on September 28 in a series of runs on the banks. On that date the *Missouri Republican* reported the closing of Darby & Barksdale and John J. Anderson. The same paper reported the closing the next day of Bogy, Miltenberger & Co. and serious runs on Boatmen's, Lucas & Simonds, and the German Savings Institution.

On September 30 the *Republican* thought that the panic was over, but it was somewhat premature in this opinion. During October it reported closings as follows: on the 3rd, Chouteau, Harrison & Valle; on the 4th, E. W. Clark & Bro.; on the 5th, Lucas & Simonds; on the 6th, the Mutual Savings; on the 19th, Tesson & Danjen; on the 21st, Renick & Peterson; on the 24th, the Bank of the State of Missouri; on the 26th, the Merchants; and on the 27th, the Southern Bank. The shock to the city attending the closing of Lucas & Simonds can hardly be over-estimated. This was probably the strongest of the private banking houses, but in thirty days it had paid out almost a million dollars. Its suspension increased the already heavy pressure on the other banks. Boatmen's experienced its worst day on October 6. The run began early that morning and lasted until closing time. The next morning the Bank published a short notice in the *Republican* which read as follows:

> "Whereas there are rumors injurious to this institution that a portion of its cash funds are on deposit in other institutions of this city, the Board deem it proper to state that *all* the cash funds belonging to it are *in its own vaults*."

The paper stated editorially that the "capacity of the [Boatmen's] Bank to meet any demand was not impaired by this demonstration, and it cannot be." The article continued to the effect that the withdrawals had not made any great impression on its holdings and that Boatmen's had refused proffered specie from other banks during the day. The latter statement may have been true, but it is unlikely that much specie was offered because the other banks were also under pressure. The State Bank remained closed only two days, being opened again on October 26, but after reopening it did not pay out specie, and this policy was gradually followed by the other banks of issue.

On October 27 Boatmen's issued a statement in which it said that it would continue to pay out in specie all deposits then on hand, and that it would continue to receive and pay out in specie, deposits made in that medium. From that date, however, all deposits made in notes of the chartered banks of Missouri would be accepted, but these notes, and not specie, would be paid out to those who had deposited them. In other words, the Bank did not propose to accept on deposit paper which was worth less than par and to pay out gold at par against such deposits. This procedure was the forerunner of the so-called "bankable fund" plan whereby the currency of the banks of issue was kept in a separate account.

By the end of October most of the tension was gone. The public felt little or no fear concerning the integrity of the banks which remained open or had resumed payments, and since currency could not be exchanged for gold at the expense of banks, it saw no purpose in indiscriminate withdrawing of deposits.

The panic had left in its wake, however, the inevitable period of stagnation, and while maturing loans were being renewed in some instances, no new loans were being made. At Boatmen's the cash account on September 8 had been $113,000. On November 10 it had grown to $508,400, all of which was in the Bank's own vaults. The statement for the end of 1857 shows loans at less than $400,000, but by July, 1858, they were up almost to $800,000, and by January, 1859, almost to $1,000,000. Railroad stock appeared in the investment account for the first time in January, 1859. This was the $10 par value stock of the Pacific Railroad of Missouri.

The banking problems brought into focus by the panic of 1857 continued to trouble St. Louis for some time. Under the Banking Act of 1857 the penalty for suspension was forfeiture of the charter. But so many banks had suspended that when the matter came up in the Legislature, it was considered expedient to nullify rather than to enforce the penalty. The Legislature thus confirmed the "bankable fund" plan and while this was unsatisfactory to many persons, it did have the virtue of practical workability. Unfortunately it was not a complete solution.

The parent banks in the city which had branches in other towns in the state found that the notes of their branches had a tendency to drift into St. Louis and when they were presented for payment at the parent bank, such payments resulted in a drain of the parent's specie while gold was left in the vaults of the branches. To protect itself on this score, in May 1858, the Bank of the State of Missouri refused to accept the notes of its own branches except as "bankable funds" and the branch bank notes immediately dropped to a discount.

Both Boatmen's and the State Savings had checks drawn on the State Bank which they presented for payment, demanding gold or city paper, i.e., the notes of the parent bank. The State Bank refused payment at par and offered notes of the branches. The savings banks then protested the checks in an effort to force the State Bank and the other banks of issue to receive branch bank notes as well as the parent bank notes at par. The State

Bank refused to do this and the other banks of issue followed their lead.

Boatmen's, the State, the Franklin, and the German Savings Institution then joined in a notice addressed to the banks of issue, which read in part:

> ". . . . . after Monday, the 2nd August, payment will be demanded in city paper or gold on all checks drawn on you received by us."

For one of the few times in its career the *Republican* criticized Boatmen's for this action, commenting that the savings banks could lend at higher interest rates and were endeavoring to secure more business by discrediting the banks of issue.

This attitude was obviously unfair to Boatmen's and the other savings banks. When Boatmen's customers received checks drawn on the State Bank and deposited them at Boatmen's, they expected to receive credit for the face amount of the checks. When Boatmen's presented the same checks at the State Bank, however, payment would be made only in paper worth a discount of 2½%. The situation had been brought about by the refusal of the banks of issue to pay their obligations at par, and the savings banks were attempting to protect themselves in a perfectly legitimate way.

The guerilla warfare which was caused by these events went on for a number of years. At one point the banks of issue caused a bill to be introduced in the Legislature to place the savings banks under the direct supervision of the bank commissioner who would then examine them.

The savings banks answered by memorializing the Legislature, saying that they had been forced by the State Bank's action to institute the "bankable fund" plan although they believed it unsound; they pointed out that there was no reason for keeping two accounts for funds on deposit since this had the effect of depreciating all Missouri currency; they cited their own records of operation and suggested the disquiet that would follow any tampering with them; they accused the bank commissioner of trying to get the savings banks under his control so that he could close them and then divert their business to the banks of issue; and they finally said that there was no reason to examine them because their transactions were not legitimately a matter of interest to the general public, since they issued no notes for circulation, but simply did business upon their own capital and their deposits, and that it was a matter of choice when any person made deposits with them. The Legislature evidently considered these arguments sound, since it did not pass the bill.

The sniping between the banks of issue, led by the State Bank, and the savings banks, led by Boatmen's continued. In order that customers of the savings banks might not suffer from the discount when they were forced to accept notes of branch banks located outside St. Louis, the savings banks made an arrangement to clear the branch bank notes among themselves, each taking the notes of the branch banks located in a particular area and sending messengers to present and collect the notes at their source of issue. Some of the experiences of these messengers were exciting, to say the least.

In the fall of 1858 William H. Thomson—who later served as Boatmen's cashier for over forty years—was sent to Liberty, Missouri, with $55,000 in notes on the branch bank located in that town with instructions to collect the notes in gold, in which they were payable. The normal procedure would have been for him to have the gold transported to the local express office and forwarded to St. Louis. There was much feeling in the country towns, however, about what was considered the draining of the specie holdings of their branch banks by the city banks.

Through some means on this particular occasion word got around town that Mr. Thomson was conducting a raid upon their bank. A mob quickly formed and Thomson was notified that if he attempted to ship the $55,000 in gold from Liberty, he would be lynched. Having delivered this warning and knowing that the stagecoach on which he expected to leave would not depart until the following morning, the mob dispersed; whereupon Thomson hired a buggy and team at the livery stable, loaded his gold and drove rapidly away, conveying the gold to the express office in the nearest town.

Incidents more or less similar to this were happening in every section of the state. A messenger from Boatmen's presenting currency at the State Bank's branch in Hannibal was tendered payment of one $5 note and refused on the balance of his presentation on the excuse that the bank was not required to pay more than one note to a holder on one day. In the general understanding of the law, this action constituted suspension of payment, for which the law provided a penalty of 20% of the amount of currency on which payment was refused.

Boatmen's counsel held this view, and the Bank brought suit to collect the penalty. Although this case was finally carried to the Supreme Court, it had languished for so long in the lower courts that the original controversy had been settled and par payment resumed before it was adjudicated.

In lending an attentive ear to the plea of the savings institutions in regard to restriction by examination, the Legislature was showing a sound sense of political values. These banks had assumed such an important position in the life of the community that an arbitrary attempt to restrict them would have been met with a storm of public disapproval. At that time the nine banks of issue and their twenty-nine branches in Missouri had less than $5,000,000 of discounts, while Boatmen's alone had $825,000. In 1859 Boatmen's bought $200,000 Missouri bonds from the State, and $20,000 short term bills of the Pacific Railroad. In addition to its commercial credits, it was financing many public and industrial projects. It was an important factor in the development not only of the Pacific, but of several other railroads.

When the Bank reached its first five-year anniversary under the new charter on January 1, 1861, the rumblings of the coming war had begun to drown out all other sound. The net profits for the five-year period were more than the Bank's capital of $400,000. In 1860 alone they had been over $100,000. But the Directors could sense trouble ahead, and even if they had previously intended to pay a dividend, which is doubtful, the outlook would have prevented such action. They decided that the profits should be retained in the Institution "for the better security of depositors and for the best interests of the stockholders."

In view of subsequent events, it was a wise decision. Discounts, which had been averaging $60,000 a week, shortly dropped below $5,000, and the Bank hurriedly made arrangements for the collection of the large amounts of southern exchange it held. Not only individuals, but the banks of issue were classified as Northern or Southern sympathizers. The expenses of the State of Missouri for military purposes began to mount, and suggestions were made that banks which had been classified as "Southern" be seized. Ignoring these suggestions, Governor Gamble requested unsecured loans. In response he received loans from the St. Louis banks aggregating $775,000. Of the total, $154,300 was from Boatmen's, only the State Bank being a larger participant. Some historians have said that these were "forced" loans, but the whole amount was repaid without controversy and nothing in Boatmen's records indicates that it was unwilling to lend its share.

Much of the business of St. Louis banks and commercial houses had been in the South, and with that territory shut off, there was little activity. The liquidation of inventories and the general stagnation is illustrated in the growth of Boatmen's deposits from approximately $1,000,000 at the end of 1861 to $2,228,000 at the beginning of 1865.

One activity that provided use for the Bank's money in this period was the continued development of the railroads. Boatmen's had many early connections with the Pacific Railroad of Missouri, later to become the Missouri Pacific. Before 1860 Hudson E. Bridge, James H. Lucas, and John M. Wimer, Directors of the Bank, had served as president of the railroad company. Of the first $200,000 of its stock subscribed, $80,000 came from Boatmen's directors. In 1859 the Bank bought $200,000 Missouri bonds from the State to provide it with funds to advance to the Pacific Railroad; in 1864 it bought $500,000 Pacific Railroad Construction Bonds, and in 1869 $321,000 of its Real Estate Bonds. In 1865 it bought from the Pacific $687,000 St. Louis County Bonds

Head Quarters, Dist. of West Tenn.

Memphis, Tenn 27th 1862

The Guards will pass Mr. R. J. Lackland
through the and back this evening on
the road leading to the South West
from the city.

U. S. Grant
Maj. Gen.
Com.

which the railroad had received from the county in payment for stock.

In the same period the Bank bought $100,000 St. Louis and Cedar Rapids, $200,000 North Missouri Railroad, and $50,000 Union Pacific Bonds; made loans of $200,000 on the Lindell Hotel, $250,000 on the Southern Hotel. When the Southern Hotel loan was not promptly paid at maturity, it was taken over by Robert Campbell who had made a large fortune in the fur trade, and is perhaps best known to present-day St. Louisans through the preservation as a museum of his house at Fifteenth and Locust Streets.

Shortly before the war began, the Bank had made a loan on some cotton below Memphis, and in 1862 it was lodged somewhere between the Union and the Confederate lines. In an effort to salvage something from it, Rufus Lackland made a trip to Memphis where on June 27 he was issued a pass through the Union lines. The pass was written in the hand of the commanding general, Ulysses S. Grant, who had been a customer of the Bank during his residence in St. Louis in the 1850s.

Many similar incidents indicate the difficulties confronting the Directors as they reached the second five-year anniversary under the current charter on January 1, 1866. In spite of the fact that St. Louis business had found it necessary to change its character completely, the profit account of the Bank showed a large total. It was the banking practice of the time to carry doubtful items suspended rather than to charge them off promptly. Some considerable part of the book profits, therefore, would not be realized, and since the Directors did not know what this would amount to, they passed their second opportunity under the "five-year plan" to declare a dividend.

The next five year period seems to have been marked by smoother sailing than the Bank had experienced up to this point. Certainly there had been enough strife and contention, financial, political and otherwise. In the late 1860s in St. Louis most persons seemed satisfied to work peacefully, which was fortunate, for there was plenty of work to be done. Discounts in the Bank rose steadily, and by 1870 the discount committee found it necessary to meet daily in order to consider the increased number of applications. Exchange on such widely separated places as New York, New Orleans, Cincinnati, Louisville, San Francisco, Chicago, Pittsburgh, Kansas City, and Mobile showed in the statement.

In 1870 a change in Boatmen's officers was occasioned by the death of Charles Hodgman who had been cashier since 1857. He had been an unusually valuable man, and in addition to a good salary, he had received a number of substantial bonuses, including a $30,000 residence. To replace him, the Board elected William H. Thomson who had entered the employ of the Bank in 1857. The choice was a fortunate one. As employee, officer and director, Thomson served the Bank for over sixty years.

The balance sheet at the end of 1870 showed:

Resources		Liabilities	
Cash	$ 408,000	Capital	$ 400,000
Exchange	468,000	Surplus.	2,033,000
Discounts. . . .	3,730,000	Profits for past 12	
Bonds and stocks .	333,000	months.	260,000
Real Estate	92,000	Bills payable. . . .	300,000
		Deposits	2,038,000
	$5,031,000		$5,031,000

The Directors felt that they had finally reached a point where a dividend could be paid. They were limited to one-quarter of the profits for the past five years, but these had been over $1,200,000, and they declared a 75% dividend, or $300,000.

Sullivan Blood had served as President since 1854, and was feeling the limitations of his age. In January, 1871, he refused re-election, but agreed to remain on the Board. An original Trustee, he had been one of the principal forces in the Board from the beginning. He had guided the Bank through the panics of 1855 and 1857 and through the troubled Civil War period. From a small savings bank with deposits impaired after the robbery in 1854, he had advanced the Institution to a position near the top of the heap. He had forced his own Board to adopt a practical basis of operation; he had crossed swords with the banks of issue in their attempt to squeeze out the "upstart" savings banks. If he had ever retreated an inch, it was only to secure firm footing from which he could again advance.

When the Directors in their testimonial mentioned Blood's "untiring zeal, constant watchfulness, high toned Gentlemanly bearing, strict impartiality, and just regard for all that is right," the words were no formal pat on the back. They were a heartfelt tribute!

V

Long Run

RUFUS J. LACKLAND, the son of Dennis and Eliza Appleby Lackland, was born in Montgomery County, Maryland, in 1819 and came with his family to Missouri in 1835. By 1837 he was a clerk on the steamboat *Clyde* in the St. Louis-New Orleans trade and later worked on other boats, including the famous *Eclipse*. In 1847 he left the river to become a member of the firm of William M. Morrison & Co., wholesale grocery dealers. Lackland was an industrious, intelligent, and pleasing young man and these qualities brought him friends and success.

In 1854 he was elected a Trustee of Boatmen's. He was one of the charter members of the Board under the 1856 charter, which membership he held until his death in 1910. In 1871 he succeeded Sullivan Blood as President. He was already president of the Gas Light Company, and was active in various other organizations.

Although during his incumbency the presidency of the Bank was a full-time job, Lackland found time during most of his career to take an active interest in other companies, notably Belcher's Sugar Refining Co., the Iron Mountain Railroad, the Oakdale Iron Works, and the Scotia Iron Co. In 1889 upon the organization of the Missouri Botanical Garden to preserve for the city the gift of Henry Shaw, Lackland became president of the Board of Trustees and retained that position until less than two months before his death.

RUFUS J. LACKLAND AND WILLIAM H. THOMSON

*Lackland was President 1871–1910. Thomson was connected with the
Bank for over 63 years. This photograph was taken
on Lackland's ninetieth birthday.*

During Lackland's presidency Boatmen's was to advance from second to first place in St. Louis banking, and then slowly see a number of other banks surpass it in size. Through all of the period the Bank gained, but in the latter years others gained faster. When Lackland became President, there was still not enough banking capital in St. Louis, and those who had money to lend could take their pick among the borrowers. Lackland felt that if he solicited a man's account, he would be under moral obligation to lend him money when he needed it, and he had no intention of placing himself under indiscriminate obligations.

Before Lackland's death conditions were reversed. There was plenty of money to be borrowed, and banks which were not in the comfortable position of Boatmen's were eagerly seeking borrowers, and finding them. He could not have failed to discern this. But even if the Bank had been making less money, he probably would not have changed his methods. As it was, the Bank was highly successful, and what did it matter if others might boast of larger totals?

Shortly after Lackland took office, the Gas Light Company opened an account, depositing $50,000, and the Bank discounted a $300,000 note for the Pacific Railroad. At the beginning of Captain Blood's administration transactions of this size would not have been possible. Lackland received a salary of $10,000, whereas Blood's had started at $1,000. The Bank was growing rapidly and once again it began to think about changes in its charter.

The current charter would expire in 1876, and the Board decided it would be unwise to approach that date too closely before seeking a new one. This time it would not be necessary to secure a special charter, but the Bank wanted to increase its capital to $2,000,000, and under the General Corporation Law in effect, that capitalization was twice as much as was permitted. Accordingly in 1872 the Bank asked the Legislature to raise the limit for banks to $5,000,000, which was promptly done. To the surprise of everyone, Governor B. Gratz Brown vetoed the measure. His message of February 28 stated in part:

> "Such immense aggregations of capital are always against public policy, and I can see nothing in the purpose of these institutions to warrant this increase."

The Directors went into action at once, and a number of prominent persons spoke to Governor Brown about the value of banks. Three days later, on March 2, he reversed himself, saying this time:

> "While such large aggregations of capital serve many useful purposes in manufacturing and mercantile commerce, yet— they are always against public policy, unless sufficient guarantees shall be constituted as will enforce detailed periodic publication of . . . . . conditions."

Thus while Boatmen's had attained its immediate objective, it had also come one step nearer examinations by the state. In attempting to secure additional privileges it had always found that they were likely to be accompanied by onerous obligations.

The plan for the new capitalization was simple. The capital funds of the Bank amounted to $2,800,000, of which $800,000 was to be paid out in a cash dividend of $200 on each $100 par value share. Then all holders who desired could exchange their old shares for new at the rate of five new for one old. Those who might want to sell were offered $500 each for the old shares. For those who had taken their stock at $100 on subscription in 1856, this meant that in addition to the $275 in dividends they had received, there was a profit of $400, or a return of 42% a year. The holders of 420 shares out of 4,000 elected to sell. Obviously the 2,100 new shares were readily placed.

The new charter, to extend over a period of fifty years, was issued in September, 1873, to The Boatmen's Savings Bank. There were eleven Directors. Sullivan Blood was the only original Trustee included. George Budd resigned just before the charter was issued, and died two years later; Luther M. Kennett had died in Paris early in 1873. Blood died in 1875, a few months after Budd, the last of the 1847 organization.

The period of the 1870s was a trying one for the banks of St. Louis. During the first three years, business had been good, but in September, 1873, the outstanding investment banker of the country, Jay Cooke & Co. of Philadelphia, failed, and a number of the New York banks suspended. This action forced the banks in many other cities to follow their lead. While St. Louis was probably less affected at the time of the panic than most other cities, the depression which followed caused deep disturbances. This was due largely to the fact that so many of the banks were not on a sound basis.

In 1875 the *Republican* listed fifty-two city bank stocks with their quotations. Fifteen of these banks had less than half of their capital paid in. Of the fifteen, only four had over 40%, and three had 15% or less; all but one of them were paying semi-annual dividends ranging from four to fifteen per cent.

When the Legislature had decided that its policy of maintaining a monopoly for the Bank of the State of Missouri was outmoded, it had caused the sale of the stock of that bank which was owned by the State, and had begun to grant charters without the safeguards which should have accompanied the privileges they carried. The depression of the Seventies began to show up the abuses which had developed under this indiscriminate chartering, and in 1877 the Legislature passed a new banking act designed to clean up the situation. Statements were required on call at irregular intervals, dividends could be paid only when earned, and capital impairment, unless promptly replaced, required liquidation.

Shortly after the passage of this act, but not because of it, the Bank of the State of Missouri closed. Under private management since 1857, the bank had taken a national charter in 1866. From that time on, apparently, it had deteriorated and shrinking values in assets in latter years had finished the job.

Other banks which had never been on a sound basis were eliminated by the provisions of the new banking act. There were sixty banks in St. Louis in 1873 and by 1879 the number had dropped to twenty-five. In the same period aggregate banking capital had dropped from $19,000,000 to $11,000,000, deposits from $46,000,000 to $30,000,000.

The State Bank closed on June 20, 1877, and this, with the public concern occasioned by the other changes which were taking place, caused runs on a number of banks. The *Republican* records the closing within the next month of the German Bank, the Butchers' and Drovers', the St. Louis Savings, the Bank of St. Louis, and the Bremen Savings.

Stronger banks were not seriously troubled. Boatmen's had begun in 1873 a program of retrenchment and revaluation of its assets, and by 1877 it could have weathered almost any storm. During that period Boatmen's deposits had increased from $3,554,000 to $4,463,000 and the percentage its capital funds bore to St. Louis' total increased from eleven to twenty.

The Bank has always been fortunate in the loyalty of its customers. An instance of this feeling is recalled in connection with the events just mentioned. During the 1877 excitement, when John J. Broderick was in the east on business, he received a letter from his mother asking his advice as to whether she should withdraw her funds on deposit at Boatmen's. He wrote in reply on July 21, telling her not to worry about her money:

> ". . . . for if that Bank is not safe, the Bank of England is not . . . . I have the most unbounded faith in (it) for had it busted, I would not have a cent."

Things of wide importance have a way of slipping unobtrusively into the course of events. If any business man today had to conduct his affairs without a telephone, he would be severely handicapped, but business had gone on at Boatmen's for thirty-one years without one. Amid the worries and tribulations of 1878 the telephone came to St. Louis. One was installed in the Bank, with the call number 19.

The period from 1880 to 1890 was probably the most colorful of any decade in Boatmen's history. The Bank had emerged from the troubled 1870s as the dominant figure in St. Louis banking, and even before 1880 the character of its business had begun to change from that of a purely local depository to one of national recognition. The signature registers of the time list names of banks and business houses from New York to San Francisco, New Orleans to Winona, Minnesota. Boatmen's had the account of the Cherokee Nation, whose headquarters were at Fort Gibson, Indian Territory, and marking the persistence of an old trade route, the Bank of Santa Fe. A number of accounts which flourished in this period have been continuously maintained since.

The archaeologist who digs in the dust of forgotten centuries has no more interesting field than the early signature registers of a pioneer bank. In Boatmen's register most persons and businesses passing through or remaining in St. Louis left their tracks. And "tracks" they were in many cases. In the early days a few wrote legibly, many atrociously, and of course, quite a few could not write at all. The latter class, signing the register with a scrawled "X," were unwittingly providing touches of humor for those who later would search these pages. In most cases, naturally, the individuals were not well known, and in order that they might be identified when they came to make withdrawals, the tellers wrote physical descriptions in the register. While the descriptions were factual and of practical use, the subjects would seldom have felt complimented. A typical one read:

> "James F———. A red-faced Mick with whiskers around his face. Works in the Lindell car barns and smells like a horse."

But if it brought the illiterate, the tide of fortune brought also the literate. On the day before he was to be married, a man wrote in Boatmen's register in a round open hand, "Eugene Field." A St. Louis County farmer and woodchopper, who would later capture both Richmond and Washington, signed, "Ulysses S. Grant"; a man concerned with transportation, "Erastus Wells." Years before, Mr. Chambers had urged the backing of "the good and the humane of the community." The Bank was receiving this backing and there is a great temptation to list not a few, but thousands of their names.

The years were bringing changes, not only to the Bank, but

AT WASHINGTON AVENUE AND FOURTH STREET

*Cashier Thomson thought it "the finest bank building in
the United States". Occupied 1891–1914.*

to the city as well. St. Louis was no longer a mere steamboat
landing. The railroads had changed that, and the Bank's location at Second and Pine Streets was being left in a backwash as
the business district moved "up on the hill," once the site of
Laclede's common fields.

In 1888 the Bank bought a lot on the northwest corner of
Fourth Street and Washington Avenue for $150,000, upon
which in 1890 it erected a seven-story building. Occupied on
March 2, 1891, this fifth location would house the Bank until
March 9, 1914. The structure cost $325,000 and was a matter
of great pride to Cashier Thomson who described it in the
fiftieth anniversary booklet as "the finest bank building in the
United States." The Bank occupied the first two floors and
basement.

During Mr. Lackland's administration there were four severe
panics. The one which began in 1873 has already been mentioned. That of 1884 touched St. Louis very lightly, and following the cleanup of the banks under the new state banking
law in 1877, found the existing banks in sound condition. The
panic of 1893 was much more severe locally. Loans were reduced radically and deposits shrank almost $25,000,000, or
about 30 per cent of the city's total. Boatmen's deposits dropped
from $6,939,000 in June, 1892, to $5,418,000 in June, 1893. In
1907 the "currency panic" was severely felt in St. Louis. The
banks made settlements among themselves with Clearing
House Certificates and many of them issued "John Smith
checks" which circulated in lieu of currency. It is a tribute to
the management of the banks and the confidence of the people
that none of the latter three disturbances caused the closing of
any banks.

On February 28, 1910, as it must to all men, death came to Rufus Lackland. He was in his ninety-first year, had become a Trustee of Boatmen's fifty-six, and its President thirty-nine years before. He had been influential as a Trustee, and as President he had virtually dominated the course of the Bank. His policies had always been sound, but he had been unyielding. He had brought Boatmen's to the top, and although its totals were about three times as large at his death as they had been when he became President, the Bank had receded in relative position in St. Louis banking. In 1880 it had had twenty per-cent of the aggregate capital funds of the city banks, but by 1910 it had only four per cent.

VI

Fire

EDWARDS WHITAKER was the first President of the Bank who had been born in St. Louis. That event took place on April 29, 1848. The son of William A. and Letitia Edwards Whitaker, he was educated in the St. Louis public schools, and his first job was helping to load and unload steamboats on the St. Louis levee. He was later an employee of the United States Sub-treasury, and the investment banking firm of Edwards & Mathews. He became a member of this firm, and the firm eventually became Whitaker and Co.

Whitaker was elected a Director of Boatmen's in 1880, Vice-President in 1895, and upon Mr. Lackland's death he succeeded to the presidency. He was a director of the Louisiana Purchase Exposition, of the Bell Telephone Co., the Missouri Electric Light Co. He was president of the Board of Trustees of the Missouri Botanical Garden, the Lindell Railway Co., the St. Louis Transit Co. and the United Railways Co. When the Chicago, Burlington and Quincy Railroad decided to enlarge its freight terminal, which involved buying land, obtaining franchises, vacating streets, and other complications, both legal and political, Mr. Whitaker made the many necessary arrangements. As president of the United Railways Co. in 1900, he personally directed the company's forces during one of the most bitter strikes the city ever experienced.

Whitaker had great faith in the eventual rehabilitation of the southern states after the Civil War. This was a controlling factor in much of his business career and contributed in a large degree to his success. The same faith, held by Rufus Lackland, formed a common meeting ground for the two men and probably accounts for their intimate and co-operative association. They had worked together closely for thirty years before Mr. Lackland's death, and the change in leadership could not have been expected to alter the fundamental policies of the Bank.

In an early statement to the newspapers, however, the newly elected President said that the outlook and methods of Boatmen's would be modernized. The changes went as far as a new set of by-laws, one section of which adjured the Directors "to foster a spirit of co-operation at all times for the advancement of the Bank's interests and the enlargement of its business." It was both admonition and admission that Boatmen's was now admittedly seeking more business. As one means to that end a rearrangement of the Bank's quarters was made which seated the executive officers in the front of the banking room instead of the rear, where they had traditionally placed themselves.

Although the newspapers commented approvingly upon these changes, they were changes in form and not in spirit. Edwards Whitaker might sit at the front, but he was the same man who had recently sat at the rear, and he retained the firm conviction that he, and no one else, should run "his" bank. Although determined and unyielding on principles, he was basically a kindly, soft-hearted man, and to protect himself from what he considered his own weaknesses, he maintained a brusque, gruff exterior which few of his acquaintances ever penetrated. In his incumbency he typified the figure which later would come to be known as the "rugged individualist."

Edwards Whitaker
President 1910–1926

Since 1903 the upper floors of the Bank building had been occupied by the Missouri Athletic Club, and on March 8, 1914, a fire started in the club quarters which destroyed the building and caused the deaths of thirty-seven persons. It became obvious through the night of March 8 that no banking could be done at the old stand the next morning, and some vacant ground floor rooms in the Pierce Building at Fourth and Pine Streets were engaged, and counters hastily built. On the morning of March 9, while the fire was still burning fiercely, the Bank opened with borrowed currency and no books. Only after six weeks was it possible to open the vaults. The books and money were found intact, but thoroughly soaked with water. A place had to be found where the books could be spread out to dry, and by coincidence that place was the old building at Second and Pine Streets which the Bank had occupied until twenty-three years before.

Although the fire obviously represented a serious financial reverse, its customers displayed no loss of confidence in the Bank. It transacted business for two months without access to individual accounts of customers with no serious controversies, and no loss. The length of time during which customers could be expected to accept the inconvenience of makeshift accommodations was limited, however, and search for a permanent location began at once.

At the corner of Broadway and Olive Street the Monward Building which had been under construction for some time was nearing completion. Part of its ground floor space had not been leased. Through this circumstance the Bank acquired the nucleus of its present location and moved in during November, 1914. The name "Monward" was dropped and that of "Boatmen's Bank Building" adopted.

The year 1914 saw the organization of the Federal Reserve System, confronting all state banks with the question of whether they should join. The advantages and disadvantages were discussed at Boatmen's and the Board authorized the necessary steps for affiliation. Although this authorization was repeated several years later, Mr. Whitaker never took those steps. Twelve years would pass and Whitaker's resignation would have been accepted before the Bank finally became a member of the system.

As far as is known, Mr. Whitaker explained to no one his reasons for his failure to join. Although his refusal to act has occasioned many questions, when his character and personality are considered, the answer seems fairly obvious. As has been mentioned, Whitaker was highly individualistic. He wanted as little supervision and regulation as possible, and operation under state laws was not as closely restricted as under Federal Reserve regulations. Moreover, there were possibilities for profit under a state charter, not open to Federal Reserve member banks. Almost continuously from 1914 to 1926 Boatmen's extended lines of credit to large customers in amounts exceeding the limitations of the Federal Reserve Act, and these were highly profitable accounts. It also carried on its books through this period more real estate than it would have been permitted as a Federal Reserve member, but this was not an important reason for failure to join since this could have been charged off at any time.

World War I disrupted operations and reduced profits, but on the whole had little effect on the Bank. Two "firsts" resulted, however, from this period. For the first time in its seventy years women appeared at its windows as tellers, and in participating in the Liberty Loans, for the first time the Bank urged upon customers the purchase of investment securities.

A landmark passed in 1920 with the death of William H. Thomson, who had entered the employ of the Bank in 1857. He had been a stalwart figure in St. Louis banking and had had no small share in Boatmen's success.

On January 19, 1926, Mr. Whitaker's resignation was accepted by the Board. He was in ill health, and his death followed on April 1. He was succeeded by Julius W. Reinholdt, the senior Vice-President. At the beginning of Whitaker's presidency the Bank's deposits had been less than $12,000,000. At his resignation they were approximately double that amount. During the same period the Bank had maintained its position in ratio of total resources to the totals of all St. Louis' banks. Six had larger totals.

The executive officers sat at the front of the banking room rather than at the rear. Typewriters were in use, but carbon paper was not. Letters were typed in indelible ink. They were then moistened and copied in a book, as on the day the bank opened. There were adding machines, but no bookkeeping machines. Although marked by a definite resistance to change, Whitaker's able management of the Bank maintained the confidence of its customers; and in spite of many unprogressive tendencies, in 1920, a time when it was much less common than now, group life insurance was provided at the expense of the Bank for all employees.

On the day it accepted Whitaker's resignation, the Board resolved to request a national bank charter. Formalities of examination, approval of the Comptroller of the Currency, and of the stockholders followed promptly. On April 9, 1926, the Bank accepted its fifth charter under the name "The Boatmen's National Bank of St. Louis." The Bank agreed to reduce within six months its thirteen excessive lines of credit. Charge-offs recommended by the Comptroller were $87,000, less than three-tenths of 1% of total resources. Even after joining the national banking system, Boatmen's did not immediately become a bank of issue. Its first notes for circulation were issued in 1932 and were retired in 1935.

The Directors may have felt, with the new charter in the vault and new signs on the front door, they could settle back in their chairs for a while and enjoy a period of ease. Such fond hopes, if entertained, soon took wing. Following World War I an inflationary trend set in, to be broken temporarily in 1921 while swollen inventories were reduced, then to resume a giddy upward spiral to be broken in the disaster of the early 1930s.

In the period between World War I and 1930, it became the conviction of many persons that the existing banks were not large enough to perform their proper functions, and since banks could grow only slowly, that there must be consolidations. Whether or not in answer to that demand, the period was marked in St. Louis by the merger of the St. Louis Union, the Mechanics-American National, and the Third National Banks to form the First National Bank in St. Louis; the Mercantile Trust Company and the National Bank of Commerce joined in the Mercantile-Commerce Bank and Trust Co.; and the Merchants Laclede National and the State National went into the Mississippi Valley Trust Co. Also, the First National absorbed the Liberty Central Trust Co., an earlier consolidation of the old German Savings Institution and the Central

National Bank, and later would take over the Franklin-American and the International Bank.

Perhaps events such as these are not of particular importance to persons not directly connected with banks, but to those in banking they naturally are of intense interest. New alignments are the offensive maneuvers of competition, must be considered as such, and necessary defensive moves made. Sometimes such arrangements come even closer, as in 1928 when articles appeared in the newspapers announcing Boatmen's imminent consolidation with the National Bank of Commerce.

An investment banking firm had accumulated a considerable amount of Boatmen's stock and proposed to the Bank the consolidation which was later announced as "practically consummated." Some of the Directors thought this might be a good idea and negotiations were carried on. At least two Directors, however, were definitely against a merger—not this one in particular, because the Bank of Commerce was a fine institution —but *any* merger. Joseph R. Matthews and Edward J. Costigan felt that the name which had gained prestige for over eighty years should be preserved; and while they did not deny that large banks might be a good thing for St. Louis, they were firm in their conviction that Boatmen's need not be one of the largest in order to continue to give satisfactory service to its customers.

As the question was discussed in Board meetings from time to time other members began to come to their side, with the result that the idea of any combination was discarded. This refusal to follow the trend left the Bank in the position of sitting and doing nothing while competitors were moving toward larger and better business. It was quite natural that since

Matthews and Costigan had defeated the move for consolidation, theirs should be the task of suggesting alternatives. Since both of them were men of sound ideas, they thought they knew what to do. Their program for equipping Boatmen's to meet heavier competition with greater growth within the Bank itself is discussed in the following chapter.

Tom K. Smith

President 1929–1947, Chairman of the Board 1947–

VII

New Crew

THE investment banking firm of Kauffman, Smith & Co. had been in business since 1915. Its Vice-President, Tom K. Smith, had been born in Glenwood, Missouri, and had come to St. Louis in the spring of 1904, following his graduation from the University of Missouri, as director of the University's exhibit at the World's Fair. When that job was finished he had gone into the office of Little & Hays, an old and respected investment house. In 1910 he had transferred his connection to the William R. Compton Co., remaining there until 1915.

Innate friendliness, a strong sense of responsibility, and a large capacity for hard work had brought him steady advancement and a wide circle of friends. In addition to his business activities, he had served as officer or board member of many organizations such as Red Cross, Children's Aid Society, Community Fund, Chamber of Commerce, the University and Noonday Clubs.

When in 1929 Directors Matthews and Costigan had come to talk to Smith they had intended to offer him a job as Boatmen's President. Before the conversations ended, they had made an arrangement to acquire the entire Kauffman, Smith organization. Most banks had investment departments of one sort or another, but Boatmen's, save for its activity in the Liberty Loan campaigns, had never offered investment securities to its customers. The Directors came to the conclusion that in addition to obtaining a general infusion of new blood, they could well meet the spirit of the times by inaugurating an investment department.

On June 1, 1929, Smith became President of the Bank, and Harold M. Kauffman President of the newly-formed Boatmen's National Company. With one exception the officers of Kauffman, Smith & Co. were elected to appropriate offices in the investment affiliate, the exception being Harold T. Jolley who became a Vice-President of the Bank.

On June 29, 1929, deposits were $23,625,000, loans were $20,590,000, and total resources $28,731,000. It will be recalled that since the financial reaction of 1921 there had been a constant inflationary trend, and while this trend still appeared strong in June, 1929, the loans at Boatmen's were receiving very close attention. While the total had been reduced less than a million dollars by the end of the year, the composition of the loan portfolio had been greatly improved.

The collapse of the stock market in October and its continued decline highlighted the shrinkage of values. The familiar pattern of previous depressions followed. Loan totals receded until in June, 1933, they were less than $8,500,000. Deposits were lower in 1930 and 1931, reaching $22,000,000 in June, 1932. From that date forward, however, they increased steadily. St. Louis had decided again that Boatmen's was a sound bank.

The crisis for the country as a whole came in the early months of 1933, when each day newspapers listed the number of banks which had closed, culminating in the bank holiday which began on March 4. There is a noticeable similarity in the local situation between the periods 1873–1880 and 1925–1935.

It has been recorded in Chapter Five that between 1873 and 1880 the number of banks in St. Louis declined from 60 to 25, and their aggregate deposits from $46,000,000 to $30,000,000. The following table shows the number of banks in St. Louis and St. Louis County and their aggregate resources at the end of the years indicated.

	Number of Banks	*Aggregate Resources*
1924	56	$738,000,000
1929	53	727,000,000
1934	32	561,000,000

At the end of 1924, 1929, and 1934, Boatmen's had ranked seventh, sixth, and fourth respectively. In 1924 and 1929 it had about 4 per cent of the aggregate resources, and in 1934 about 8 per cent. Emphasizing the effect of the mergers of the 1920s, 85 per cent of the aggregate resources at December 31, 1934, were in the first four banks. The first three were together the repositories of some twenty-five bank charters. Only Boatmen's had had no consolidations.

With changing economic conditions St. Louis had a larger proportion of industrial population in 1932 than that with which it had faced the depressions of 1873 and 1893. In common with other centers of large population the city confronted the problem of widespread destitution. Tom K. Smith had been appointed St. Louis member of the National Organization on Unemployment Relief by President Hoover, a member of the Missouri Committee on Unemployment Relief by Governor Caulfield, and Chairman of the St. Louis Committee on Relief and Employment by Mayor Miller.

Although administering relief in any crisis is a difficult task, the bleak days of 1932 presented an acid test. In this delicate situation it was Smith's responsibility to represent the national, state, and city governments, and the people, to see that none should starve . . . that every able person should contribute his full share . . . that bitterness arising from fear and suspicion, stalking constantly in the near background, should not break into open strife. Short tempers and raw nerves needed soothing.

In a special campaign Smith's committee raised $1,200,000 for relief, in a year when money was scarce, and when the regular charity campaigns had already been held. The situation required a firm and steady hand at the controls to assure donors that contributions would not be wasted, recipients that they were not being neglected. When the city had passed through this crisis and orderly procedure had been restored, Smith received recognition unusual in its timeliness and scope.

An anonymous citizen of St. Louis had established a fund and an award to be made annually to the St. Louisan who during the year had performed the most creditable service for the city. The first award under this grant was made in 1932, and Smith received it.

In an amendment to the Banking Act, the 1933 Congress made illegal the operation of securities affiliates. Conforming to this change, the Boatmen's National Company was liquidated and a bond department was organized to carry on in the Bank such of its functions as the amended law permitted.

Also in 1933 Congress made provision for the temporary insurance of bank deposits. The already overburdened Treasury staff lacked the wide acquaintance with local banking conditions which implementation of this provision required. To remedy this lack, in November the Secretary of the Treasury invited Smith to come to Washington.

Boatmen's had emerged from the banking holiday with no serious problems, and the Board was not only willing, but eager to do anything that might help toward recovery from the critical situation into which the business of the country had been forced. It felt, moreover, that in Washington, Smith would be able to do a great deal toward the re-establishment of cordial relations between the banking industry and the administration.

Although the Secretary's invitation raised several serious questions, these were solved by the Board's generous decision to grant Smith a leave of absence, and to lend his services to the Treasury as long as they might be needed. The Treasury accepted this arrangement and Smith was given the title of Special Advisor to the Secretary on Banks and Banking Matters.

Smith's wide knowledge of banking conditions and his numerous friendships in the industry greatly simplified the problem of putting the temporary deposit insurance into operation. At the beginning of 1934, when that job was finished, the office of Under Secretary of the Treasury had fallen vacant and the Secretary offered Smith the appointment. For the same reasons which a few months before had forced him to decline an official appointment, he could not accept. He agreed, however, to remain until a suitable man could be found for the post.

Between the first of the year and the end of May, Smith served on many of the important Treasury committees, represented the Treasury at the Reconstruction Finance Corporation, and participated in the discussions of the future of deposit insurance. These discussions developed what has become an important part of the banking system, first through an extension of the temporary insurance, and the eventual creation of the Federal Deposit Insurance Corporation. Smith also served as consultant on those phases of the Securities and Exchange Act related to Treasury financing and commercial banking. In May, with the warm commendation of the Secretary of the Treasury, he returned to St. Louis.

The Board's belief that Smith could establish a better relationship between the banks and the administration had been justified. A letter from the President said:

THE WHITE HOUSE

WASHINGTON

May 24, 1934

Dear Tom:

As I have told you, it is with real and deep regret that I let you return to St. Louis. If I were not a sympathetic soul, the Marines would have prevented your departure. You have done splendid service not only for me but for the country, and I am deeply grateful.

Remember that this is only a holiday for you and that I count on your being back with us again.

Always sincerely,

Franklin D. Roosevelt

Hon. Tom K. Smith
President of the Boatmen's National Bank
St. Louis, Missouri

In the operation of the temporary deposit insurance, where banks lacked sufficient capital, the arrangement was that capital would be supplied by the Reconstruction Finance Corporation, in most cases through the purchase of preferred stock. A serious objection to this arrangement developed from the fact that if one bank in a community sold preferred stock to the R. F. C., it was thereby marked as a weak bank and the confidence of its customers would be shaken. To avoid this, the Treasury asked many patently sound banks to sell stock to the R. F. C. so that no stigma might attach to those who sold stock under necessity. In co-operation with this program, Boatmen's sold $500,000 of preferred stock to the Reconstruction Finance Corporation. At the same time the par value of the common stock was reduced from $100 to $20 and the holders received four new shares for one old. The preferred stock was retired in 1936, out of earnings, and in October, 1941, a 25 per cent stock dividend was declared, restoring the common capital to $2,500,000. In May, 1945, another stock dividend brought the capital to $3,000,000.

The American Bankers Association had realized the importance to the banking business of the work which Tom Smith had done in Washington, and at its annual convention in October, 1934, elected him Second Vice-President. In the usual succession Smith was elected President in 1936. Also in 1936 F. Lee Major, a Vice-President of the Bank, served as President of the Missouri Bankers Association, and in 1943 David L. Colby, Assistant Vice-President, was elected President of the American Institute of Banking.

At the end of 1942, deposits had passed $100,000,000. The Bank was organized for broadened activities and was benefiting from them. In addition to his duties in the Bank, Smith was taking an active part in local and national civic matters, as President of the Board of Curators of the University of Missouri, as Chairman of the St. Louis Social Security Commission, as Chairman of the National Citizens' Committee on Mobilization for Human Needs, and member of the board of National War Fund, Inc. At the same time he served on the

Boards of the American Telephone and Telegraph Co., the General American Life Insurance Co., the Wabash Railroad Co., and the Federal Reserve Bank of St. Louis.

Active participation of the United States in World War I had been short enough that many businesses were very little affected, but in World War II the necessary adjustments and additional effort disturbed almost every organization down to its foundations. At the end of 1940 the Bank had 28 women employees. At the end of 1945 this number had grown to 159. Two-thirds of its male employees of military age entered the armed services, others went into war industries. Operation at a normal level with a staff of lowered average experience is difficult enough, and Boatmen's might very well have chosen to seek no new business during the war years and to ride through "comfortably."

Instead, the Bank sought every opportunity to take on extra work if that work promised to help in the war effort. Payroll accounts of large war industries, not considered particularly attractive by many banks, were actively sought and obtained. Special credit arrangements were made to enable manufacturers to convert to war production. The entire Bond Department was assigned to the task of selling War Bonds, with resulting sales of over $350,000,000 to more than 150,000 persons and businesses during the war period. Of the four banking facilities established on military posts in Missouri, Boatmen's operated the two largest. These were only the larger activities; there were innumerable others.

President Roosevelt's prediction in 1934 that Smith was only being allowed a holiday when he returned to St. Louis was borne out. He was recalled to Washington in 1939 and 1940 as special advisor to the Treasury, and in 1942 and 1943 as financial advisor to the office of Procurement and Material of the Navy Department.

In addition to its coverage of group life insurance, the Bank announced on February 1, 1941, the inauguration of a group annuity plan for the retirement of over-age employees and has since added hospitalization, and medical, surgical, and diagnostic X-ray aid.

In 1945, looking toward post-war developments, a department was started for making small loans payable in installments, a step reminiscent of Mr. Budd's original conception of the Bank, and in 1946 in a more modern vein, a parking lot was provided for the free use of customers while transacting business with the Bank.

Civic service at Boatmen's has not been confined to its top officers. The entire staff, with the encouragement of the management, participates in as many activities as possible. As a result of its part in the 1946 Community Chest Campaign, it received a plaque with the citation:

> "In presenting this Plaque to the Boatmen's Bank, I would like to call your attention to the fact that 100% of their employees contributed. It was not only 100% this year, but for many, many years they have participated on this basis toward our Chest Campaign. Their past performance is one of our best examples of outstanding citizenship."

In its first ten years the Bank outgrew three locations and each time solved the problem by moving to larger quarters. In 1891 it moved to Fourth Street and Washington Avenue because the business district had shifted. Forced to leave that place when the building was destroyed by fire, it came to

Broadway and Olive Street, originally taking about half of the first and second floors and some basement space. It has been necessary at about ten-year intervals since 1914 to make major alterations to take care of increasing business. Following the most recent remodeling, completed in 1947, the Bank occupies the basement and first four floors of the building which bears its name.

At the annual meeting in January, 1947, Tom K. Smith was elected Chairman of the Board, remaining active as the chief executive officer. During his presidency of over seventeen years the Bank's deposits had increased from $24,000,000 to $120,000,000. It remained the fourth bank in size and had 7 per cent of St. Louis' aggregage bank resources.

The share of St. Louis' total bank resources held by the first four banks had been 85 per cent on December 31, 1934; on December 31, 1946, it was 66 per cent. Resources tend to concentrate in times of stress, and to be redistributed as conditions ease.

To succeed Smith, the Board elected Harold T. Jolley as its seventh President. He had come into the Bank in 1929 as Vice-President in charge of public relations. Born in St. Louis August 21, 1889, he had attended the St. Louis public schools and was graduated from the University of Missouri. His business experience had been gained in wholesale merchandising and investment banking.

In addition to his duties in the Bank, for a number of years he had taken an active part in civic, charitable, and political affairs. He had served as board member or officer of the St. Louis Chapter of the American Red Cross, the St. Louis Board of Election Commissioners, the Mercantile Library Association, the Episcopal Home for Children, The Home of the Friendless,

HAROLD T. JOLLEY

President 1947–

the Automobile Club of Missouri, the Bryan Mullanphy Emigrant and Travellers' Relief Fund, the Governmental Research Institute, the Jefferson National Expansion Memorial Association, United Charities, Inc., the Municipal Theatre Association, the St. Louis War Chest, and the Base Hospital Unit Number 21 Memorial Trust Fund.

Also in January, 1947, Albert Wagenfuehr was elected Chairman of the Executive Committee, a newly created position. He was employed by the Bank from March, 1911 to August, 1913, when he resigned to accept a position with a cotton brokerage firm. He returned to the Bank in February, 1915, and has been since that time a member of the Credit Department. He was elected Assistant Cashier in 1921 and Vice President in 1926. As head of the Credit Department since 1918 he has been responsible for its organization in its current form. He is a charter member of the Robert Morris Associates, the national organization of bank credit men, and since its organization, has been active in its work.

VIII

Conclusion

GEORGE BUDD had worked very hard to build up the organization which sponsored the little bank, and on October 18, 1847,
he was immensely proud of it. Someone else may have seen
only wooden counters in a converted jewelry store. Budd saw
an institution that would benefit the community. The processes
of change have affected the town that he chose for his home and
have affected the Bank. The busy scene on the levee, which attracted Budd on the day he arrived in St. Louis, is gone; but the
river carries far more freight tonnage than it did a century ago.

Gone, too, are the pine counters, the bearded tellers, from
the Bank; but the Bank is carrying more traffic as well. The
quill pen of Treasurer Simpson no longer scratches over pon-
derous ledgers. Records are posted by machine and by photog-
raphy. Throughout the year temperature and humidity are
measured and controlled.

The Bank is doing many things for its customers which the
early depositors would not have expected. Trust and bond departments serve corporate and individual customers.

If Mr. Budd could return on October 18, 1947, he would
doubtless be amazed at the changes. But he could still feel the
pride that was his on the first day. After 100 years the Bank is
still receiving deposits "from Boatmen, and from others." It is
still providing credit for the community and for the individuals
who compose it.

APPENDICES

Appendix A

Boatmen's Trustees and Directors
1847–1947

Name	Term Began	Terminated
B. W. Alexander	February 16, 1847	September 14, 1847
Thomas Andrews	February 16, 1847	April 27, 1853
Henry D. Bacon	February 16, 1847	September 9, 1847
James G. Barry	February 16, 1847	September 20, 1847
Sullivan Blood	February 16, 1847	November 27, 1875
George Knight Budd	February 16, 1847	September 29, 1873
Samuel C. Davis	February 16, 1847	April 13, 1848
Edward Dobyns	February 16, 1847	April 23, 1850
Luther M. Kennett	February 16, 1847	April 12, 1873
Adam L. Mills	February 16, 1847	February 6, 1856
Daniel D. Page	February 16, 1847	September 9, 1847
Laurason Riggs	February 16, 1847	September 14, 1847
George W. Sparhawk	February 16, 1847	April 20, 1848
Amedee Valle	February 16, 1847	December 3, 1850
John M. Wimer	February 16, 1847	May 29, 1857
A. H. Glasby	September 9, 1847	May 15, 1855
Asa Wilgus	September 9, 1847	March 23, 1865
John F. Darby	September 14, 1847	March 20, 1851
Edward Haren	September 14, 1847	April 20, 1848
A. B. Chambers	September 23, 1847	May 24, 1854
August Brewster	April 20, 1848	March 20, 1851
Alexander Kayser	May 2, 1848	January 3, 1849
Peter Brooks	May 16, 1848	October 17, 1848
Joseph Throckmorton	November 7, 1848	March 20, 1851
Robert Holmes	February 20, 1849	July 16, 1863
Hudson E. Bridge	May 21, 1850	December 19, 1854
William D'Oench	June 1, 1853	May 3, 1859
Rufus J. Lackland	June 28, 1854	February 28, 1910
Carlos S. Greeley	January 23, 1855	April 13, 1898
Louis A. LaBeaume	May 29, 1855	March 31, 1871
Adolphus Meier	November 30, 1855	December 31, 1884

93

Name	Term Began	Terminated
James Smith	February 22, 1856	October 15, 1877
James H. Lucas	April 6, 1858	January 8, 1872
George S. Drake	May 27, 1859	January 17, 1907
William M. Morrison	January 5, 1864	August 1, 1865
William A. Hargadine	January 11, 1867	January 4, 1892
John G. Copelin	January 10, 1868	December 30, 1871
E. J. Glasgow	April 1, 1871	June 6, 1879
W. P. Howard	January 8, 1872	January 14, 1879
John B. C. Lucas	January 8, 1872	January 14, 1879
William H. Thomson	August 2, 1873	June 23, 1920
John Whittaker	January 10, 1876	January 14, 1879
E. C. Simmons	January 14, 1878	March 25, 1895
L. L. Butler	January 13, 1879	March 31, 1882
Theodore Forster	January 13, 1879	January 9, 1883
Theophile Papin	January 13, 1879	June 19, 1879
Samuel Cupples	January 26, 1880	January 15, 1901
Edwards Whitaker	January 26, 1880	January 11, 1926
Jerome Hill	January 9, 1883	December 30, 1896
William L. Huse	January 14, 1884	December 23, 1901
George E. Leighton	January 12, 1885	July 4, 1901
George P. Whitelaw	January 11, 1892	January 30, 1892
R. McKittrick Jones	January 9, 1893	August 7, 1912
Byron Nugent	January 13, 1896	April 4, 1908
E. O. Stanard	January 13, 1896	January 8, 1912
Murray Carleton	January 9, 1899	November 19, 1925
George J. Tansey	January 14, 1901	January 11, 1905
W. K. Bixby	January 13, 1902	January 9, 1906
William G. McRee	January 13, 1902	January 11, 1906
D. S. H. Smith	January 13, 1902	July 18, 1915
Louis Werner	January 12, 1903	January 15, 1907
Hanford Crawford	February 28, 1905	September 20, 1912
F. E. Sheldon	January 14, 1907	January 18, 1928
Samuel D. Capen	January 13, 1908	January 28, 1933
Henry W. Peters	January 11, 1909	October 14, 1916
Ernest M. Hubbard	January 9, 1911	January 11, 1915
W. K. Stanard	January 8, 1912	August 3, 1934
Clarence H. Howard	August 9, 1912	January 11, 1916

Name	Term Began	Terminated
William G. McRee, Jr.	January 13, 1913	January 15, 1913
Samuel W. Fordyce	July 25, 1913	January 12, 1915
Jesse L. Carleton	January 11, 1915	January 11, 1916
Nelson G. Edwards	January 11, 1915	January 10, 1922
Clarence R. Laws	January 11, 1915	September 23, 1918
H. B. Collins	January 10, 1916	August 2, 1916
Aaron Waldheim	January 10, 1916	January 9, 1934
Joseph R. Matthews	January 14, 1918	
Edgar L. Taylor	January 13, 1919	January 28, 1945
Julius Glaser	January 12, 1920	March 20, 1941
Julius W. Reinholdt	January 12, 1920	January 10, 1933
Alexander Robertson	January 10, 1921	April 6, 1923
Albert T. Terry	January 10, 1921	February 1, 1947
Maurice Wright	January 9, 1922	June 17, 1930
Benjamin F. Bush	January 11, 1926	July 29, 1927
Edward J. Costigan	January 19, 1926	January 9, 1935
Leroy C. Bryan	January 11, 1927	June 7, 1934
Charles Gilbert	January 11, 1927	December 1, 1937
T. O. Moloney	June 1, 1927	
Herman C. Stifel	January 10, 1928	February 25, 1929
J. Hugo Grimm	January 8, 1929	October 4, 1929
Harold M. Kauffman	May 28, 1929	March 1, 1934
Tom K. Smith	May 28, 1929	
Walter M. Smith	October 4, 1929	October 29, 1931
E. E. Pershall	June 17, 1930	
W. C. Henning	January 9, 1934	
F. Lee Major	January 9, 1934	June 29, 1942
Albert Wagenfuehr	January 9, 1934	
John S. Lehmann	August 1, 1934	
Charles Belknap	January 14, 1936	
Alvin Griesedieck	January 10, 1939	
William L. Holley	January 10, 1939	July 31, 1945
Harold T. Jolley	January 13, 1942	
Frank E. Agnew	November 13, 1945	
Harry F. Harrington	January 14, 1947	
Royal D. Kercheval	January 14, 1947	
Robert W. Otto	January 14, 1947	

APPENDIX B

BOATMEN'S OFFICERS

1847–1947

Chairman of the Board

Name	Term Began	Terminated
Julius W. Reinholdt	June 1, 1929	January 10, 1933
Tom K. Smith	January 15, 1947	

Vice-Chairman

Aaron Waldheim	June 1, 1929	January 9, 1934

President

Adam L. Mills	September 9, 1847	June 14, 1854
Sullivan Blood	June 14, 1854	January 6, 1871
Rufus J. Lackland	January 9, 1871	February 28, 1910
Edwards Whitaker	March 8, 1910	January 11, 1926
Julius W. Reinholdt	January 12, 1926	June 1, 1929
Tom K. Smith	June 1, 1929	January 15, 1947
Harold T. Jolley	January 15, 1947	

Chairman of the Executive Committee

Albert Wagenfuehr	January 15, 1947	

Vice-President

George S. Drake	January 8, 1871	March 6, 1895
Edwards Whitaker	March 6, 1895	March 8, 1910
Murray Carleton	March 8, 1910	November 19, 1925
William H. Thomson	January 10, 1911	June 23, 1920
Julius W. Reinholdt	January 13, 1914	January 12, 1926
C. R. Laws	January 12, 1915	September 23, 1918
Aaron Waldheim	January 14, 1918	June 1, 1929
Edgar L. Taylor	January 14, 1919	January 28, 1945
Leroy C. Bryan	January 11, 1921	June 7, 1934
Benjamin F. Bush	January 12, 1926	July 29, 1927
J. Hugo Grimm	January 12, 1927	January 20, 1931

96

Name	Term Began	Terminated
F. Lee Major	January 12, 1927	June 29, 1942
Albert Wagenfuehr	January 12, 1927	January 15, 1947
Harold T. Jolley	January 15, 1930	January 15, 1947
Alfred Fairbank	January 14, 1931	March 3, 1938
Harold M. Kauffman	January 9, 1934	March 1, 1934
Royal D. Kercheval	January 9, 1934	
W. Glenn Rule	January 14, 1936	
Harry F. Harrington	March 16, 1937	
H. F. Hagemann, Jr.	March 15, 1938	August 3, 1946
Clarence D. Cowdery	January 10, 1940	
Arthur F. Boettcher	January 12, 1944	
W. Gillespie Moore	January 12, 1944	
David H. Morey	January 12, 1944	
Paul H. Young	July 1, 1945	
David L. Colby	February 12, 1946	

Cashier

Alton R. Easton	December 22, 1855	March 11, 1856
Charles Hodgman	March 18, 1856	April 23, 1870
William H. Thomson	May 17, 1870	January 10, 1911
Ernest M. Hubbard	January 10, 1911	January 11, 1915
Julius W. Reinholdt	January 11, 1916	January 12, 1926
Leroy C. Bryan	January 12, 1926	June 7, 1934
H. Alfred Bridges	January 9, 1935	March 31, 1945

Secretary

Benjamin B. Chamberlain	September 20, 1847	April 23, 1850
Joseph W. Thornton	May 21, 1850	November 28, 1854
John D. Taylor	December 5, 1854	December 22, 1855

Treasurer

Robert Simpson	September 16, 1847	June 29, 1854
Alton R. Easton	June 29, 1854	December 22, 1855

Assistant Vice-President

Lawrence Boogher	January 15, 1930	April 18, 1939
H. Fred Hagemann, Jr.	January 9, 1934	March 15, 1938

Name	Term Began	Terminated
W. Gillespie Moore	January 9, 1934	January 12, 1944
W. Glenn Rule	January 9, 1934	January 14, 1936
Robert W. Stumpe	January 9, 1934	January 29, 1938
Cecil C. Combs	December 18, 1934	
Arthur F. Boettcher	January 14, 1936	January 12, 1944
David L. Colby	January 25, 1938	February 12, 1946
C. C. Hammerstein	January 25, 1938	March 31, 1945
Clement T. Kelly	January 25, 1938	
David H. Morey	March 18, 1939	January 12, 1944
Carroll E. Gunnin	October 21, 1941	
Robert R. Heslep	January 13, 1943	
Kenneth A. Bell	January 12, 1944	
Julius W. Schwaig	January 12, 1944	
W. Paul Harper	February 12, 1946	

Assistant Cashier

Name	Term Began	Terminated
William H. Thomson	October 26, 1869	May 17, 1870
William A. Clendenin	January 15, 1884	November 12, 1894
Jules Desloge	November 27, 1894	June 13, 1906
E. M. Hubbard	June 19, 1906	January 10, 1911
Edgar L. Taylor	January 10, 1911	January 14, 1919
Leroy C. Bryan	January 9, 1917	January 11, 1921
H. Alfred Bridges	January 14, 1919	January 9, 1935
Rudolph Felsch	January 14, 1919	August 1, 1941
C. C. Hammerstein	January 14, 1919	January 25, 1938
Albert Wagenfuehr	January 11, 1921	January 12, 1927
Oliver Knippenberg	January 12, 1927	July 13, 1935
Fred E. Blomberg	January 14, 1936	
Clement T. Kelly	January 14, 1936	January 25, 1938
Julius W. Schwaig	January 14, 1936	January 12, 1944
Bert A. Lynch	January 10, 1940	June 21, 1941
Richard L. Maguire	October 21, 1941	
Raymond Meckfessel	October 21, 1941	
Robert A. Niemann	January 12, 1944	

Name	Term Began	Terminated

2nd Assistant Cashier

Name	Term Began	Terminated
Jules Desloge	April 23, 1891	November 27, 1894
E. M. Hubbard	November 27, 1894	June 19, 1906
Edgar L. Taylor	June 19, 1906	January 10, 1911
C. R. Laws	January 10, 1911	January 12, 1915

Trust Officer

Edgar L. Taylor	January 12, 1927	January 28, 1945
Alfred Fairbank	January 14, 1931	March 3, 1938
Royal D. Kercheval	March 15, 1938	
Clarence D. Cowdery	January 10, 1940	
David H. Morey	January 12, 1944	

Assistant Trust Officer

Edgar H. Bohle	January 14, 1936	September 15, 1944
Clarence D. Cowdery	January 14, 1936	January 10, 1940
Robert L. Fornshell	January 25, 1938	June 30, 1946
Hugh S. Hauck	January 10, 1940	
Clifford H. Albers	January 12, 1944	April 30, 1947
John G. Neugebauer	January 10, 1945	

Auditor

Rudolph Felsch	November 1, 1915	January 14, 1919
William J. Jones	January 1, 1919	January 1, 1922
Lloyd E. Woods	January 10, 1922	April 6, 1928
Harry F. Harrington	May 1, 1928	March 16, 1937
Wilson P. Jeannelle	March 16, 1937	

Real Estate Loan Officer

George Stolz	January 14, 1936	

Appendix C

ACT PASSED BY THE GENERAL ASSEMBLY OF THE STATE OF MISSOURI AND APPROVED FEBRUARY 16, 1847

AN ACT TO INCORPORATE THE BOATMEN'S SAVING INSTITUTION

WHEREAS the Boatmen and other industrious classes of the City of Saint Louis, need an Institution in which they can safely deposit at interest, their earnings, and experience has proved that saving institutions have been productive of great benefit to the laboring classes, inducing habits of economy and industry: Therefore,

Be it enacted by the General Assembly of the State of Missouri, as follows:

1—George W. Sparhawk, Sullivan Blood, Edward Dobyns, Luther M. Kennett, Daniel D. Page, B. W. Alexander, Adam L. Mills, Amedee Valle, George K. Budd, Thomas Andrews, Henry D. Bacon, Laurason Riggs, Samuel C. Davis, James G. Barry, John M. Wimer, and such others as shall be elected by them, shall be a body corporate and politic, by the name of the "Boatmen's Saving Institution," and by that name shall be incorporated for twenty years from the passage of this act, provided the legislature may repeal this act at any time. The above named persons shall constitute a board of Trustees of this Institution and they or a majority of the board, shall always have power to fill any vacancies that may occur in this body: They shall elect a President from their own body and may appoint a Treasurer and such other officers and agents as may be necessary. If any officer, clerk or agent of the institution shall appropriate the funds of the Institution to his own use, or the use of others, without authority of the trustees, it shall be deemed a misdemeanor, and on conviction he shall be punished by fine, or imprisonment, or both. Any two of the Trustees may call the others together to organize the Institution.

2—Said corporation may have a common seal, which they may change at pleasure, and all deeds, grants, and agreements made by the Treasurer or Cashier, or by any other person by their authority and direction according to their instructions shall be good and valid; and the said corporation shall at all times have power to sue and be sued, implead and be impleaded, and defend by the name aforesaid.

3—Said corporation shall be capable of receiving from persons who are Boatmen, and from others on deposit, all sums of money that may be offered, and for which Interest may be allowed, in accordance with the by-laws of the board of trustees; and each depositor shall receive a book in which shall be entered all sums deposited.

4—To secure the corporation from loss, the money deposited shall be loaned on the following securities, to wit: On Productive Real Estate within the limits of the State of Missouri, not exceeding one-half the actual cash value thereof; provided said loans shall be the first lien on the same; or the funds may be invested in such other Stocks as may be deemed perfectly secure and which can readily be converted into money.

5—The board of Trustees shall have power to make by-laws for the management of the business of the corporation; provided the same are not repugnant to the constitution and laws of the country, and said corporation may purchase and hold Real Estate for the transaction of their business, not exceeding the value of Twenty Thousand Dollars.

6—In case of closing the Institution by a repeal of its act of Incorporation, or by forfeiture, or lapse of time, should there be any funds on hand, or real estate over and above the expenses of the Institution, it shall be equitably divided pro-rata among those persons who have had constantly on hand from the end of six months after the Institution has opened, the sum of One Hundred Dollars and upwards.

7—It shall be the duty of the Trustees—any seven of whom shall be a quorum—to publish under affidavit of the treasurer, in at least two newspapers in Saint Louis: First, the amount of funds invested, and in what Stocks; the amount loaned on Real Estate; Second, the amount on deposit on the day of publication; and Third, the amount which has been deposited since the last publication, and similar accounts shall be laid before the General Assembly during every regular session of that body.

8—The Trustees shall not be liable for losses that may accrue, without misconduct on their part; provided loans shall be made and instruments executed by them in the manner aforesaid; and they shall require the Treasurer to enter into bonds in a sufficient sum, not less than Five Thousand Dollars, with good Security, for the faithful performance of his duties.

This Act to take effect from its passage.

NOTE: There are some differences in spelling, punctuation, and capitalization in the Act as it appears in the journal of the General Assembly and as Secretary Chamberlain copied it in the Bank's Record Book A. The former version has been used here, on the assumption that it is a true copy as read to the members of the General Assembly before its passage.

Appendix D

The by-laws, as they existed at the opening of the Bank on October 18, 1847, were:

Sec. 1. That the Boatman's Saving Institution shall be composed of fifteen Trustees, one President, one Treasurer and one Secretary. The board shall elect their President from their own body, and fill vacancies in said board, and shall appoint a Treasurer and Secretary and such other officers and agents as may be deemed necessary, and the officers shall hold their offices for one year, unless sooner removed, and until their successors are duly appointed; Provided no officer shall be removed, except by a majority of the whole number of Trustees; viz, fifteen.

Sec. 2. The regular meetings of the Trustees of this Institution shall be held on the first and third Tuesdays of each month at 3 o'clock P. M.

Sec. 3. The smallest deposit shall be One Dollar, and the lowest sum which will be put upon Interest shall be Five Dollars and no fractional part of a dollar shall be received on deposit.

Sec. 4. The Institution will be opened daily (Sunday and public fasts and holidays excepted) from 10 A.M. to 4 P.M. and on Saturdays until 6 P.M.

Sec. 5. Depositors offering to deposit any funds with this Institution shall be furnished with a Book at their expense, on the first inside page of which book shall be printed, all those sections of the By-Laws of this Institution having special reference to deposits made in the same and also the terms for and upon which the depositor desires to deposit his money, which printed Copy shall be signed by the depositor and Secretary, and shall serve as evidence between this Institution and the depositor.

Sec. 6. Money deposited on Interest can only be drawn out by the depositor, or some person by him legally authorized, by a written order or check, and accompanied with the deposit book.

Sec. 7. The regular days for drawing out money at Interest, are the third Wednesdays of October, January, April and July, written notice being given one week previous, and no sum less than Ten Dollars can be withdrawn, unless the whole sum deposited by such person shall be less than that amount. Persons who deposit must sign the rules and agree to conform to them: this is necessary for the security of all parties.

SEC. 8. All depositors making deposits in this Institution shall state to the Treasurer whether he designs the money to draw Interest, or whether the deposit is liable to draft at any time.

SEC. 9. Dividends, or Interest may be received either personally, or by order in writing of depositors or by letter of attorney on producing the book of deposit.

SEC. 10. No Trustee shall receive directly or indirectly any pay or emolument for his services.

SEC. 11. Upon the death of any depositor, the money standing to his or her credit, shall be paid his or her legal representative.

SEC. 12. For the year commencing with the opening of this Institution, Interest at the rate of three per cent per annum will be allowed, on all deposits made in conformity with these By-Laws. Twice in every year, namely on the second Wednesday of April and October after October 1847, a dividend of payment of Interest of one and a half per cent, or one dollar and a half on a hundred, will be made.

SEC. 13. Those who do not take their Interest when due, will have it added to their principal on the first day of the succeeding month, after such dividend has been declared, and thus receive compound Interest on such amounts.

SEC. 14. Deposits made at any time between the first day of each month and the succeeding month, will not be put upon Interest untill the commencement of the month succeeding the deposit. The reason of this is, that it would be impracticable to compute Interest upon numerous deposits, commencing from many different periods.

SEC. 15. To secure the Corporation from loss, the money deposited shall be loaned on the following securities to wit: On productive Real Estate within the limits of the State of Missouri, not exceeding one half the actual Cash Value thereof, provided Said loans shall be the first lien on the same, or the funds may be invested in such other stocks as may be deemed perfectly secure, and which can readily be converted into money.

SEC. 16. No deposits will be received except in Gold and Silver, and notes of the Bank of the State of Missouri: provided no foreign coin purporting to be of the value of Twenty Five cents and Twelve and a half cents, shall be received at over Twenty Cents and Ten cents Value.

SEC. 17. The Trustees shall be at Liberty to return all or any part of the deposits whenever they may think proper by giving a weeks notice.

SEC. 18. All notices in relation to deposits, or depositors published in one or more of the daily papers of the City of Saint Louis shall be deemed and taken as actual notice to each depositor.

SEC. 19. Untill otherwise ordered, loans shall only be made on the first and third Tuesdays of each month and then only by the concurrence of seven of the Directors and no loans shall be made on Real Estate without the Title is clear and undisputable, which in every instance shall be certified to by the legal counsellor of the Institution; which certificate shall go on file and the Expense thereof shall be paid by the party applying for the Loan.

SEC. 20. The Treasurer and Secretary may sit in the board when convened, to give information, but in no case shall they be entitled to a vote, the directors alone being responsible for the government of the Institution.

SEC. 21. No deposits will be received from Males on Fridays this day being Expresley set apart for the female Community.

SEC. 22. No person shall be elected a Trustee or officer unless nominated at least one stated meeting before the election and the election shall be held by ballot.

SEC. 23. Any motion to amend the By Laws shall be made at the previous meeting of the board to be adopted by a majority of the whole Board.

Defining the duty of the President

1. The President may convene the board at any time he may deem proper.

2. He shall have the general supervision and control of the Institution, and his Instructions to the officers shall be binding, in the absence of instructions from the board, provided they are not contrary to the Charter and By-Laws.

Defining the duty of the Treasurer

1. The Treasurer shall have a general charge of the Cash, Funds, and papers of the Institution and when money is on deposit, other than in the Institution, the President shall sign the checks, which shall be countersigned by the Treasurer, and the same shall be registered by the Secretary that no error shall occur.

2. He shall keep in a book to be provided for, separate accounts of all and every kind of funds which may belong to the Institution, in such order as may enable the President and board of Trustees at once to verefy the exact situation of the same, and he shall also conform to such other rules and regulations as may from time to time be enjoyned upon him by resolution of the board.

3. He shall receive and enter all deposits, and pay all checks of depositors on the Institution in conformity with the By-Laws, and in no case shall he deviate from the rules and regulations for the government of the Institution.

4. All papers relating to loans, and also certificates of Stock, and all other securities, shall be under his particular charge of the Treasurer, and these papers shall be kept in a Tin Box by themselves and the Key held by him.

5. All bills for current expenses shall be audited by him and paid by order of the President alone.

6. Salaries when paid shall be paid quarterly (monthly) and in no case shall any officer of the Institution, draw his salary in advance or overdraw it, neither shall they loan the funds of the Institution for any temporary purposes to any one, this shall be a misdemeanor.

7. The Treasurer shall give bonds with at least two good securities, which shall be approved by the board of Trustees, and these bonds shall be renewed annually, and the amount extended and additional security asked if deemed expedient, to wit on the 3rd Wednesday of October of each year.

8. The President and all other officers shall be elected or re-elected annually by a formal vote of the board, "to wit, on the 3rd Wednesday of October (or as soon thereafter as may be) in each year excepting the

year 1847, provided no officer shall be elected by less than a majority of the whole board viz 15.

9. The bonds of the Treasurer for the year commencing in October, 1847 shall be ten thousand dollars and for the succeeding years not less than ten thousand dollars.

10. The Institution being an experiment at its commencement both the Treasurer and Secretary shall serve without any pledge of salary on the part of the Directors, until such time as the funds of the Institution will warrant the board allowing one, when the amount shall be defined for each of these officers.

Defining the duty of the Secretary

1. The Secretary shall be the Book-keeper of the Institution, and shall open its books, which must be kept by double-entry, in a clear and legible hand and neat manner.

2. He shall open and close the Institution and attend at the Institution daily during the time named in the By-Laws, and shall study to be affable and pleasant to all its patrons, but shall encourage no one to remain in the Institution beyond the time necessary to transact their business.

3. The Cash account of the Institution shall be balanced daily at the close of business, and the money counted, and if not found to agree, shall immediately be reported to the President, and it shall be carefully placed in the vault of . . . until otherwise ordered.

4. Depositors accounts drawing no Interest and subject to draft at any time shall be kept constantly posted as far as time will allow them to be done, and a Trial Balance of the Books of the Institution shall be made weekly untill otherwise ordered.

5. The books of the Institution shall be open to the inspection of the President and Trustees (any one of them) and the Treasurer at all times, and once a fortnight "to wit, on the first and third Tuesdays of each month, a committee of three of the board shall examine the books, and count the Cash on hand and certify to its actually being in the Institution or on deposit elsewhere.

6. The funds of the Institution are sacred and under the control only of the board, therefore any directors attempting to borrow money from the

Treasurer or Secretary without the knowledge of the board otherwise than in the manner and form prescribed by the charter, it shall be the officers duty to report such persons to the President, and it shall be the duty of the President to report the same to the board without any delay.

7. The Keys of the Institution shall be in charge of the Secretary untill otherwise ordered.

8. For the present year commencing in October 1847 the Secretary shall give bond with two good securities to be approved by the board in the sum of Five Thousand dollars and this bond shall be renewed annually "to wit, on the third Wednesday in October and the amount increased and additional security ordered if deemed expedient by the board.

9. Order and system is enjoined on all officers of this Institution, and as all whether officers or Trustees are exercising a high and benevolent trust all must be prudent and vigilent.

NOTE: The first set of by-laws was adopted at a meeting held on September 2, 1847. At a subsequent meeting they were completely rewritten, and then were amended in six instances before October 18, 1847.

They were written in the Bank's Record Book A, together with the rules defining the duties of the President, the Treasurer, and the Secretary, by Secretary Chamberlain, and are reproduced as he wrote them.